COLLECTIBLE GLASSWARE from the 40's 50's 60's...

Second Edition

an illustrated value guide

by Gene Florence

COLLECTOR BOOKS

A Division of Schroeder Publishing Co., Inc.

ABOUT THE AUTHOR

Gene Florence, born in Lexington in 1944, graduated from the University of Kentucky where he held a double major in mathematics and English. He taught nine years in Kentucky at the junior high and high school levels before his glass collecting "hobby" became his full-time job.

Mr. Florence has been interested in "collecting" since childhood, beginning with baseball cards and progressing through comic books, coins, bottles and finally, glassware. He first became interested in Depression glassware after purchasing an entire set of Sharon dinnerware at a garage sale for $5.00.

He has written several books on glassware: *The Collector's Encyclopedia of Depression Glass* in its eleventh edition; *Kitchen Glassware of the Depression Years*, in its fourth edition; *Elegant Glassware of the Depression Era*, in its fifth edition; *The Collector's Encyclopedia of Akro Agate*; *The Collector's Encyclopedia of Occupied Japan*, Volumes I, II, III, IV and V; *Very Rare Glassware of the Depression Years*, Volumes I, II and III; and the *Pocket Guide to Depression Glass*, now in its eighth edition. He recently completed the sixth edition of his innovative alphabetized *Standard Baseball Card Price Guide* that has been very well received in those circles.

Should you be in Lexington, he is sometimes found at Grannie Bear Antique Shop located at 120 Clay Avenue. Beginning in 1994, the shop will be open on Friday and Saturday only. The shop (site of his mother's former day care business) derived its name from the term of endearment toddlers gave her. In recent days he has been spending most of his time in Florida where his writing is an easier task without the phone ringing every five minutes — and fishing is just out the office door!

If you know of any unlisted or unusual pieces of glassware in the **patterns shown in this book,** you may write him May-October at Box 22186, Lexington, KY 40522, and November-April at Box 64, Astatula, FL 34705. If you expect a reply, you must enclose a SASE (self-addressed, **stamped** envelope) — and be patient. His writing, research and travels often cause the hundreds of letters he receives weekly to backlog. He appreciates your interest, however, and spends many hours answering your letters when time and circumstances permit. Remember that SASE! He does not open all that mail. Most letters without SASE are never read by him!

On The Cover: Front: King's Crown water goblet $12.00; Swanky Swigs (Tulip #3) $3.50 each; Emerald green jelly $35.00; Royal Ruby tumbler (plain) $6.50 (with ad) $12.00; Fiesta Forest green tumblers $12.00 each. Back: English Hobnail punch bowl set $300.00.

Additional copies of this book may be ordered from:

COLLECTOR BOOKS
P.O. Box 3009
Paducah, Kentucky 42002-3009

or

GENE FLORENCE

(May 1- Oct. 31)
P.O. Box 22186
Lexington, KY 40522

(Nov. 1- April 30)
P.O. Box 64
Astatula, FL 34705

@$19.95. Add $2.00 for postage and handling.

Copyright: Gene Florence, 1994.

ACKNOWLEDGMENTS

Thanks to readers, collectors and dealers who have kept me informed with new information on patterns in this book and *The Collector's Encyclopedia of Depression Glass*! All this enlightenment has added an additional forty-eight pages of new patterns and information to create a second edition of the *Collectible Glassware from the 40's, 50's, 60's...* in only two years!

Thanks to Cathy, my wife, who, over twenty-two years of writing, is still my chief editor and critic. She tries to make my writing into sentences that tell you what I meant to say as I struggle trying to type my ten words a minute. Many times it is difficult to continue a line of thought with interruptions from the phone and any of the other multitude of daily interferences that occur. (I have had two phone calls and one neighbor ringing the door bell since I started this paragraph!) It has been easier writing this book in Florida since Cathy has been here to help than it was with her being in Kentucky last time.

A special thanks to "Grannie Bear," my Mom, who spent hours wrapping, listing, and packing glass for numerous photography sessions we had for this book. She and Dad even helped in pricing since they've been making weekend excursions to flea markets and shops in our area. Also, my Dad has spent many an hour washing all the glassware! It has been quite a task just keeping glass that I have purchased divided into different photography categories: Elegant, Depression, 1950's and Kitchenware.

Thanks, too, to Cathy's Mom, Sibyl, who helped Cathy sort, pack and repack glass for days and days and to Dad, Charles, Sibyl and Marc who kept everything under control at home while we traveled. Marc has even had to take over book shipments from time to time along with his college courses. Chad will be married and graduating from the University of Kentucky by the time you read this; but he's still been around to unload and load photography glass. It's taking all hands on deck (and then some) to keep these books current, and available to you on a regular basis.

Glass, catalogues and pricing information for this book were furnished by collectors and dealers from all over the country. Among these wonderful people are: from Illinois, Dick and Pat Spencer, Floyd Craft; from Michigan, Teri Steele and Jill Farnsworth; from Missouri, Gary and Sue Clark, and Evelyn Rhoades; from Texas, John and Maria Tebbetts; from Ohio, Dan Tucker and Lorrie Kitchen, Fred Bickenheuser, Sam and Becky Collings, Ralph Leslie, Len and Arlyn Ols; from Oklahoma, Charles and Peggy McIntosh; from Washington, Carrie Domitz; from Kansas, Thomas Smith Jr.; from Massachusetts, John Benkowski; from Alabama, Kathryn Forest; from North Carolina, Dale Starnes; from Pennsylvania, Dean and Mary Watkins; from Kentucky, Jackie Morgan, Gwen Key, Gladys and Gene Florence, Sr. Additional information came from numerous readers from across the U.S.A., Canada, England, Puerto Rico, New Zealand and Australia! Please know I am appreciative! Even some information given that I can't yet use is still much appreciated — and filed.

Photographs for the book were made at Curtis and Mays Studio in Paducah by Tom Clouser and by a new cameraman, Richard Walker of New York who provided numerous photographs during a six day session that about killed our working crew from Collector Books. Glass arranging, unpacking, sorting, carting and repacking was accomplished by Dick and Pat Spencer, Lisa Cash, Sherry Kraus, Lisa Stroup, Cathy Florence and the guys from the shipping department at Collector Books. Everyone helping at these sessions wonders if we are ever going to finish. Our two van loads of glass and additional glassware brought in by friends filled an entire room with boxes. Even I had a hard time figuring out how we could get all these pictures done in the time available without someone losing his sanity. Of course, I haven't spoken to the new photographer since those six twelve hour days last October!

Thanks for all your measurements and the photographs confirming new discoveries! It takes photographs to confirm new pieces. If you have trouble photographing glass, take it outside in natural light, place the glass on a neutral surface and forget the camera has a flash attachment. A cloudy bright day works best. If you wish them returned, please enclose SASE (self addressed **stamped** envelope) that is large enough to send back your pictures. Often the SASE to send back the picture has been smaller than the photographs!

Thanks to Beth Ray in the Editorial Department at Collector Books. She turned my computer writings into actual pages of a book. There are some advantages to not yet knowing how to use their programs! It is difficult enough to keep up with all the new software updates that come out between books without learning publishing skills too!

FOREWORD

While I was writing the eighth edition of *The Collector's Encyclopedia of Depression Glass* I found that I had no room to expand to additional patterns being gathered without going over my 224-page restriction that we hold to try to keep the price of the book down. I had an idea for information on newer glassware that is now this book. The concept has gone through transitions from the initial notion; but basically, *Collectible Glassware of the 40's, 50's, 60's...* covers glassware made **after** the Depression era that is being collected by glass enthusiasts. This necessitated patterns made after 1940 being removed from *The Collector's Encyclopedia of Depression Glass* (except for a few patterns overlapping the time periods of both books). This not only gave me a platform to explore newer glass being collected but allowed me to expand *The Collector's Encyclopedia of Depression Glass* by removing non-Depression era glassware.

It took five years to put the first book into a working format, but it has now been accepted to the point that Depression Show promoters have been calling and asking me how to rewrite contracts to make allowances for glassware made in this era. Before this book, there was little information available for collectors on glassware from this period.

I am including mass produced and handmade glassware from this era since both types are being sought. A few of the glassware patterns included were begun near the end of the 1930's, but the main production of these was the 1940's, 1950's or even later.

Fire-King and Anniversary have always been thought of as Depression Glass, but neither pattern was introduced until after 1940. I have spent considerable time compiling available information on Fire-King lines. I have included examples of most Fire-King patterns that were mass marketed through the early 1960's. There are other lines made after this period that I will perhaps include later.

Fenton had few dinnerware lines introduced before 1940, so I have included some of their lines made after then.

I have also continued to add company catalogue pages of many patterns shown in this book. Thanks for all the letters confirming that you like that idea. This way most of the pieces are identified for those collectors who want to know what each piece is.

I have added new patterns that you have requested; so let me know what additional patterns you would like to see included in the next edition. I am only scratching the surface of this vast time period, but it is a start! If you have collections from this era you'd be willing to lend for photography purposes or copies of glass company advertisements you received with your sets listing pieces, let me hear from you about those.

Collectors' demand and their accumulating proclivities will determine the direction the book will take in the future. This is a response to the present direction I see collectors taking. It will probably take a few more editions to make this book's format standard. I hope you learn from it and take pleasure from it! Keep writing me of your finds! I try to pass along your information and I enjoy hearing from you.

PRICING
ALL PRICES IN THIS BOOK ARE RETAIL PRICES FOR MINT CONDITION GLASSWARE. THIS BOOK IS INTENDED TO BE ONLY A GUIDE TO PRICES AS THERE ARE SOME REGIONAL PRICE DIFFERENCES WHICH CANNOT REASONABLY BE DEALT WITH HEREIN.

You may expect dealers to pay from forty to fifty percent less than the prices quoted. Glass that is in less than mint condition, i.e., chipped, cracked, scratched or poorly molded, will bring only a small percentage of the price of glass that is in mint condition. Since this book covers glassware made from 1940 onward, you may expect that dealers and collectors will be less tolerant of usage marks or wear than glass made earlier.

Prices are fairly well standardized due to national advertising carried by specialized antique publications and dealers who attend Antique Glass Shows held from coast to coast. However, there are still some regional differences in prices due partly to glass being more readily available in some areas than in others. Too, companies distributed certain pieces in some areas that they did not in others. Generally speaking, however, prices are about the same among dealers from coast to coast.

Prices tend to increase dramatically on rare items and, in general, they have increased as a whole due to more and more collectors entering the field (and people becoming more aware of the worth of Depression and 1950's Glass).

One of the more important aspects of this book is the attempt made to illustrate as well as realistically price those items that are in demand. The desire was to give you the most accurate guide to collectible glass patterns available.

MEASUREMENTS
All measurements are taken from company catalogues or by actually measuring each piece itself, if no catalogue lists were available. Capacities of tumblers, stemware and pitchers are always measured to the very top edge until nothing more can be added to it. Heights are measured perpendicular to the bottom of the piece, and not up a slanted side. Plate measurements in company catalogues were usually rounded to the nearest inch or half inch, across the widest point; and this creates problems, today, when we go for exactness!

TABLE OF CONTENTS

ANNIVERSARY JEANNETTE GLASS COMPANY, 1947-49; late 1960's - mid 1970's

Colors: Pink, crystal and iridescent.

The acceptance of *Collectible Glassware from the 40's, 50's, 60's ...was* extraordinary! It startled both my publisher and me! As stated in the first edition, I realized that there was a need for a book that covered the glassware made beyond the Depression era while working on the eighth edition of *The Collector's Encyclopedia of Depression Glass*; but it took almost five years to make that book a reality. In only two years time the book has expanded by thirty-three percent!

Of course, I had a couple of dealers mention that I was making a mistake with this book because many patterns such as Anniversary have always been considered to be Depression glass. I disagreed because I said all along that although **some patterns have been collected as such, they truly are not**. Anniversary, though previously purchased by Depression Glass collectors, was never made during that time.

Pink Anniversary was only listed in Jeannette catalogues from 1947 until 1949; but crystal and iridescent could be purchased in boxed sets in "dish barn" outlets as late as 1975. I have seen more and more iridescent Anniversary displayed at flea markets and antique malls, but little of this later color has been allowed into most Depression era glass shows since is considered too recently manufactured. However, the iridescent is collectible and even "asked for" at shows. Be aware that iridescent is sometimes priced as if it were Carnival glass by unknowledgeable "dealers." Iridescent Anniversary actually fetches prices of pink.

I accidentally omitted the iridescent candlesticks from the last book; thanks for the letters pointing out that omission!

Crystal Anniversary is harder to find than pink or iridescent, as many collectors of crystal have found out; but it is generally not as eagerly sought.

The pink butter dish, pin-up vase, candy dish, wine glass and sandwich plate are difficult to find. In crystal those pieces are not as difficult to find. That pin-up vase is similar to the old Model T car vases that some collectors are seeking. Fresh flowers were placed in the early cars to make them more acceptable to passengers.

The bottom to the butter is harder to find than the top. This holds true for many other patterns that have heavy lids and flattened or thinner bottoms. Note the bottom is almost "plate-like." There are several styles of aluminum lids found on the crystal cake plate. No, I have no idea which is the "correct" one. Glass companies did not make metal lids, but sold the bottoms to someone who made the tops by special order.

I still get letters about the word comport after all these years. The Jeannette catalog from 1947 lists the open, three-legged candy as a comport and not a compote. They mean the same thing. Terminology has simply changed over time. Today, we usually think of a compote as a single footed dish.

	Crystal	Pink	Iridescent		Crystal	Pink	Iridescent
Bowl, 4⅞", berry	3.50	6.50	4.00	Cup	4.00	7.50	4.00
Bowl, 7⅜", soup	7.00	15.00	6.50	Pickle dish, 9"	4.50	10.00	7.00
Bowl, 9", fruit	9.50	20.00	12.00	Plate, 6¼", sherbet	1.75	3.00	2.00
Butter dish bottom	12.50	25.00		Plate, 9", dinner	5.00	10.00	6.00
Butter dish top	13.50	25.00		Plate, 12½",			
Butter dish and cover	26.00	50.00		sandwich server	6.00	12.00	8.00
Candy jar and cover	20.00	40.00		Relish dish, 8"	5.00	10.00	6.50
Cake plate, 12½"	6.50	15.00		Saucer	1.50	2.50	1.50
Cake plate				Sherbet, ftd.	3.50	7.50	
w/metal cover	15.00			Sugar	3.00	7.50	5.00
Candlestick, 4⅞" pr.	16.00		20.00	Sugar cover	6.00	10.00	3.00
Comport, open,				Tid-bit, berry & fruit			
3 legged	4.00	10.00	5.00	bowls w/metal hndl.	13.00		
Comport, ruffled,				Vase, 6½"	13.00	27.50	
3 legged	5.00			Vase, wall pin-up	14.00	25.00	
Creamer, footed	4.00	9.00	5.50	Wine glass, 2½ oz.	7.50	15.00	

"BEADED EDGE" (PATTERN #22 MILK GLASS) WESTMORELAND GLASS COMPANY, late 1930's-1950's

"Beaded Edge" is a collector's name for Westmoreland's Pattern #22 milk glass. Note that the catalogue sheet shown on page 11 shows a red decorated edge which Westmoreland called a "rich coral red." According to them, "this pattern is also hand decorated in a full dinner or luncheon service in a series of eight matching fruit designs, and it is also made without decoration."

The creamer and sugar shown with cherries on the bottom of page 9 are the same sugar and creamer shown with blueberries on the bottom of page 10. Rotating these to the other side reveals the other fruit which was a time saving decorating idea for Westmoreland. The sugar and creamer shown actually belong to another Westmoreland line (Pattern #108) and not Beaded Edge, but the fruit decorations make it a great item to go with the fruit decorated Beaded Edge. If you collect either one of these fruit patterns, I suggest you find a set of these Pattern #108 instead of the normally found footed ones, shown in the catalogue on page 12. Note that these "patterns" were **numbers** and not the "names" that collectors are so fond of using. This is true of many company's glassware lines. You can find each of the eight fruit designs in the photos on page 9 and the bottom of page 10.

The 12" platter, 15" torte plate and three-part relish remain the key pieces to find in any of the decorated lines. There are also eight floral designs depicted on the tumblers below; but, as you can see, I have only found four of the matching plates. One of the more popular decorations with collectors today is the birds. I see a few of these in my travels, but the dealers who own them usually like them more than I. You can see a red bird along with a variety of other decorations on the top of page 10. Additionally, I have included a couple of other catalogue listings on pages 12 and 13. Not one letter replied negatively to use of catalogue pages in the first *Collectible Glassware from the 40's, 50's, 60's ...*; so I have included more in this second edition. Enjoy!

	Plain	Red Edge	Decorated
Creamer, ftd.	11.00	13.00	17.50
Creamer, ftd. w/lid #108	16.50	22.50	27.50
Cup	6.00	8.00	12.00
Nappy, 5"	4.50	6.50	16.00
Nappy, 6", crimped, oval	7.00	10.00	18.00
Plate, 6", bread and butter	5.00	7.00	10.00
Plate, 7", salad	7.00	10.00	13.00
Plate, 8½", luncheon	7.00	10.00	13.00
Plate, 10½", dinner	12.00	17.50	28.00
Plate, 15", torte	18.50	32.50	45.00
Platter, 12", oval w/tab hndls.	18.50	32.50	45.00
Relish, 3 part	22.50		
Salt and pepper, pr.	20.00	25.00	35.00
Saucer	3.00	4.00	6.00
Sherbet, ftd.	6.50	10.00	16.00
Sugar, ftd.	12.50	15.00	17.50
Sugar, ftd. w/lid #108	16.50	22.50	27.50
Tumbler, 8 oz., ftd.	8.00	12.00	17.50

Please refer to Foreword for pricing information

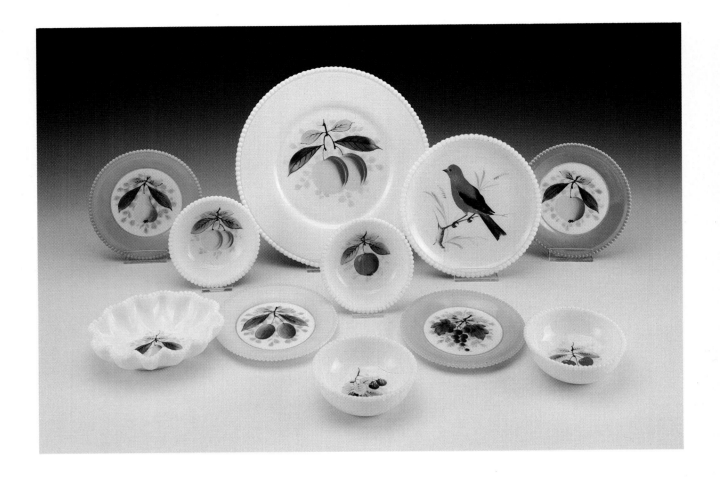

America's Finest Handmade Milk Glass

The Lazy Susan breakfast, so cheerful and so companionable, is an occasion where the mood of leisure and the friendly atmosphere of informality are complemented by the sparkle and intimate loveliness of Westmoreland authentic handmade early American Milk Glass reproductions.

Illustrated in natural color is the handmade Beaded-edge pattern with the narrow row of beads hand decorated in rich coral red. This pattern is also hand decorated in a full dinner or luncheon service in a series of eight matching fruit designs, and it is made without decoration.

WESTMORELAND GLASS COMPANY
GRAPEVILLE, PENNSYLVANIA

Handmade Glassware of Quality

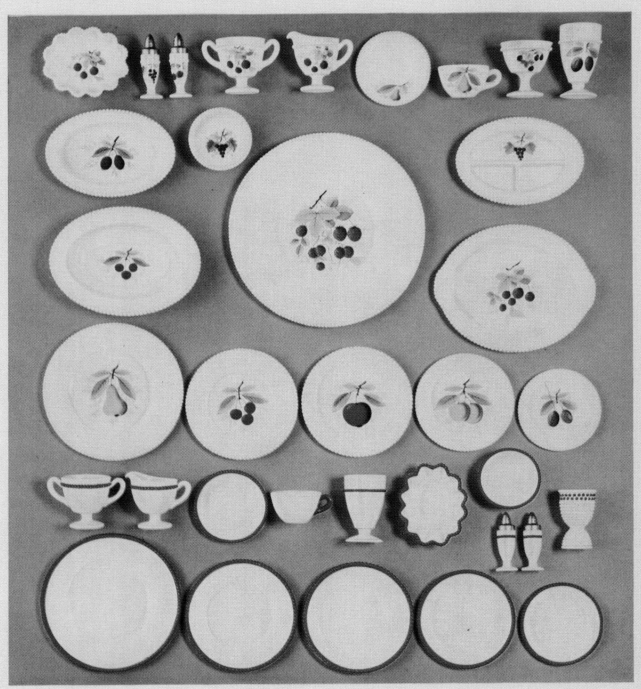

Top Row: *No. 22/6"/64-2. Oval crimped Nappy, "Beaded Edge." Note: all items are available in a set of eight different hand painted fruit decorations: Grape, Cherry, Pear, Plum, Apple, Blackberry, Strawberry and Peach, or in any fruit decoration specified above.*

No. 22/64-2. Salt and Pepper.

No. 22/64-2. Cream and Sugar.

No. 22/64-2. Cup and Saucer.

No. 22/64-2. Sherbet, low foot.

No. 22/64-2. Tumbler, footed.

Second Row: *No. 22/64-2. Celery Dish, oval.*

No. 22/5"/64-2. Nappy, round.

No. 22/15"/64-2. Plate, torte.

No. 22/3part/64-2. Plate, relish, 3-part.

Third Row: *22/64-2. Dish, vegetable.*

No. 22/12"/64-2. Platter, oval.

Fourth Row: *No. 22/10½"/64-2. Plate, dinner.*

No. 22/8½"/64-2. Plate, luncheon.

No. 22/1/8½"/64-2. Plate, luncheon, coupe shape.

No. 22/1/7"/64-2. Plate, salad, coupe shape.

No. 22/6"/64-2. Plate, bread and butter.

Fifth Row: *No. 22/A-28. Cream and Sugar, coral red "Beaded Edge" pattern.*

No. 22/A-28. Cup and Saucer.

No. 22/A-28. Tumbler, footed.

No. 22/6"/A-28. Nappy, oval, crimped.

No. 22/5"/A-28. Nappy, round.

No. 22/A-28. Salt and Pepper.

No. 77. Egg Cup, "American Hobnail" with coral red decoration.

Bottom Row: *No. 22/10½"/A-28. Plate, dinner.*

No. 22/8½"/A-28. Plate, luncheon.

No. 22/1/8½"/A-28. Plate, luncheon, coupe shape.

No. 22/1/7"/A-28. Plate, salad, coupe shape.

No. 22/6"/A-28. Plate, bread and butter.

(The "Red-Beaded Edge" pattern is also available in torte plate, platter, relish, vegetable dish and celery.)

Handmade, Hand Painted Fruit, Bird and Floral Plates

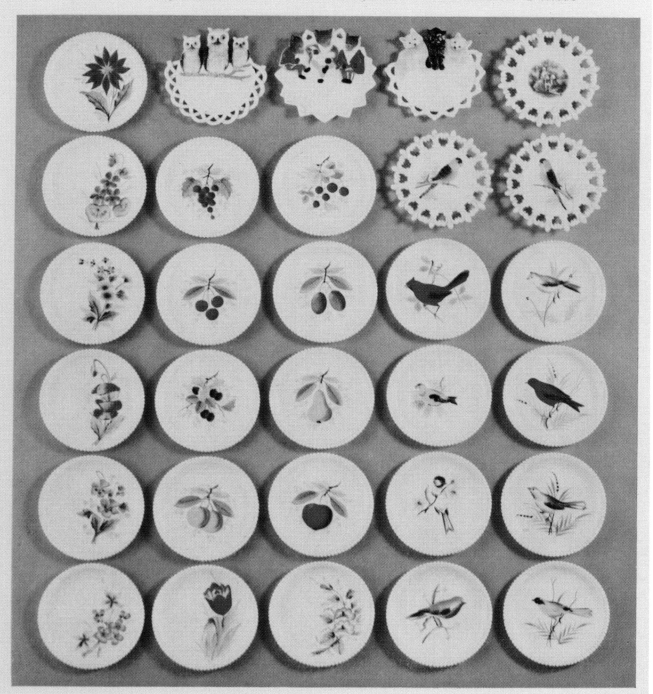

Any of the hand painted Floral, Bird, and Fruit designs shown above on "Beaded-Edge" dessert plates are available on No. 22/15" torte plate shown on opposite page. A set of eight salad plates and footed tumblers, and a 15" torte plate make an attractive luncheon or bridge set.

Top Row: *No. 22/1"/7"/4. Coupe shape, dessert or salad plate, with Poinsettia decoration. One of eight hand painted floral designs as illustrated below: Violet, Yellow Daisy, Poppy, Pansy, Apple Blossom, Tulip and Morning Glory.*

No. 6/7"/4. Plate, "Three Owls" decoration.

No. 24/7"/7. Plate, "Three Bears" decoration.

No. 5/7"/1. Plate, "Three Kittens" decoration.

No. 4/7"/WFD. Plate, "Fleur-de-lis," hand applied decal, French, Watteau Scene.

Second Row, second item: *No. 22/1"/7"/64-2. Coupe Shape dessert or salad Plate, with Grape decoration. One of eight hand painted fruit designs as illustrated at right and below: Strawberry, Cherry, Plum, Blackberry, Pear, Peach and Apple.*

No. 4/7"/76 B-R. Fleur-de-lis Plate with hand painted Parakeet (facing right).

No. 4/7"/76 B-L. Fleur-de-lis Plate with hand painted Parakeet (facing left).

Third Row, fourth item: *No. 22/1"/7"/70. Coupe Shape dessert or salad Plate, with Cardinal decoration. One of eight hand painted bird designs as illustrated at right and below: Titmouse, Goldfinch, Scarlet Tanager, Chickadee, Mocking Bird, Bluebird and Yellow Warbler.*

"BUBBLE," "BULLSEYE," "PROVINCIAL" ANCHOR HOCKING GLASS COMPANY, 1940-1965

Colors: Pink, Sapphire blue, Forest Green, Royal Ruby, crystal and any known Hocking color.

Bubble is the introductory pattern for many novice collectors! Its abundant supply of blue cups, saucers and dinner plates makes this pattern readily found and easily recognized. The simple, circular design blends well with many of today's decorating schemes. Although basic pieces are abundant in blue, other items are in shorter supply. Creamers have always been scarce, but the 9" flanged bowl has virtually disappeared from the collecting scene. You can see this bowl on the right back of the photo atop page 15. Fortunately, it is standing up so you can see the flanged rim. Do not confuse this 9" bowl with the 7¾" soup bowl as has happened before!

Forest Green (dark) and Royal Ruby (red) dinner plates have both become difficult to find. It's hard to believe that in the late 1970's a Georgia dealer found a warehouse filled with Royal Ruby dinner plates and tidbit trays and today they are difficult to find! At his original price of $3.00 each for dinner plates, it took the collecting world several years to recover from such a quantity. Today, a find like that could make you feel like a lottery winner! Many people use the red and green Bubble for their Christmas tables.

Pink is hard to find in any piece other than the 8⅜" bowl that still sells in the $5.00 range. The inside depths of these bowls vary.

That 8⅜" berry bowl can be found in almost any color that Anchor Hocking made (including all the opaque and iridescent colors common to Hocking). Milk White was only listed in the 1959-60 catalogue, but they must have been prolific in those two years since so many of them still exist today.

The other stemware line that was sold along with Bubble, shown on the bottom of page 16, has been called "Boopie" by collectors. The Royal Ruby "Boopie" is still priced about the same as the "Bubble stemware," but the Forest Green "Boopie" is selling for less than the Forest Green "Bubble stemware" shown on page 19.

According to one Anchor Hocking catalogue, the Bubble stemware was actually called "Early American" line. Both of these were made after production of blue had ceased; so, there are no blue stems to be found. Sorry!

The catalogue lists an iced tea in "Boopie" with a capacity of 15 oz.; but all we have actually been able to put in one is 14 oz!

The original labels on the crystal Bubble on the bottom of page 15 read "Heat Proof." In fact, a 1942 ad guaranteed this "Fire-King" tableware to be "heat-proof," indeed a "tableware that can be used in the oven, on the table, in the refrigerator." Presumably since this ad is dated 1942, they are referring to the light blue color. This added dimension is unique to "Fire-King" since most Depression glass patterns will not hold up to sudden changes in temperature. The Forest Green or Royal Ruby Bubble does not proclaim these heat-proof qualities, however!

	Crystal	Forest Green	Light Blue	Royal Ruby
Bowl, 4", berry	4.00		14.00	
Bowl, 4½", fruit	4.50	6.00	11.00	8.00
Bowl, 5¼", cereal	5.00	11.00	12.00	
Bowl, 7¾", flat soup	6.50		15.00	
Bowl, 8⅜", large berry (Pink-$6.00)	6.50	12.00	16.00	16.00
Bowl, 9", flanged			295.00	
Candlesticks, pr.	15.00	25.00		
Creamer	5.50	10.00	32.00	
*Cup	3.50	6.00	4.00	7.00
Lamp, 3 Styles	40.00			
Pitcher, 64 oz., ice lip	60.00			55.00
Plate, 6¾", bread and butter	2.00	4.00	3.00	
Plate, 9⅜", grill			19.00	
Plate, 9⅜", dinner	6.00	18.00	7.00	18.00
Platter, 12", oval	9.00		16.00	
**Saucer	1.50	5.00	3.00	5.00
***Stem, 3½ oz., cocktail	4.00	10.00		10.00

	Crystal	Forest Green	Light Blue	Royal Ruby
***Stem, 4 oz., juice	4.50	10.00		10.00
Stem, 4½ oz., cocktail	4.00	12.50		12.50
Stem, 5½ oz., juice	5.00	12.50		12.50
***Stem, 6 oz., sherbet	3.00	6.00		7.00
Stem, 6 oz., sherbet	3.50	9.00		9.00
***Stem, 9 oz., goblet	7.00	10.00		12.50
Stem, 9½ oz., goblet	6.00	13.00		12.00
***Stem, 14 oz., iced tea	7.00	14.00		
Sugar	6.00	10.00	14.00	
Tidbit, 2 tier				35.00
Tumbler, 6 oz., juice	3.50			8.00
Tumbler, 8 oz., 3¼", old fashioned	6.00			16.00
Tumbler, 9 oz., water	5.00			9.00
Tumbler, 12 oz., 4½", iced tea	12.00			12.00
Tumbler, 16 oz., 5⅞", lemonade	14.00			16.00

*Pink - $100.00
**Pink - $40.00
***Boopie

Please refer to Foreword for pricing information

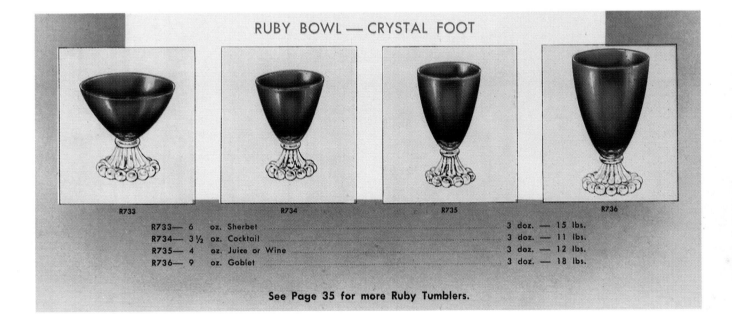

RUBY BOWL — CRYSTAL FOOT

R733	R734	R735	R736

R733— 6 oz. Sherbet		3 doz. — 15 lbs.
R734— 3 ½ oz. Cocktail		3 doz. — 11 lbs.
R735— 4 oz. Juice or Wine		3 doz. — 12 lbs.
R736— 9 oz. Goblet		3 doz. — 18 lbs.

See Page 35 for more Ruby Tumblers.

Royal Ruby Anchorglass

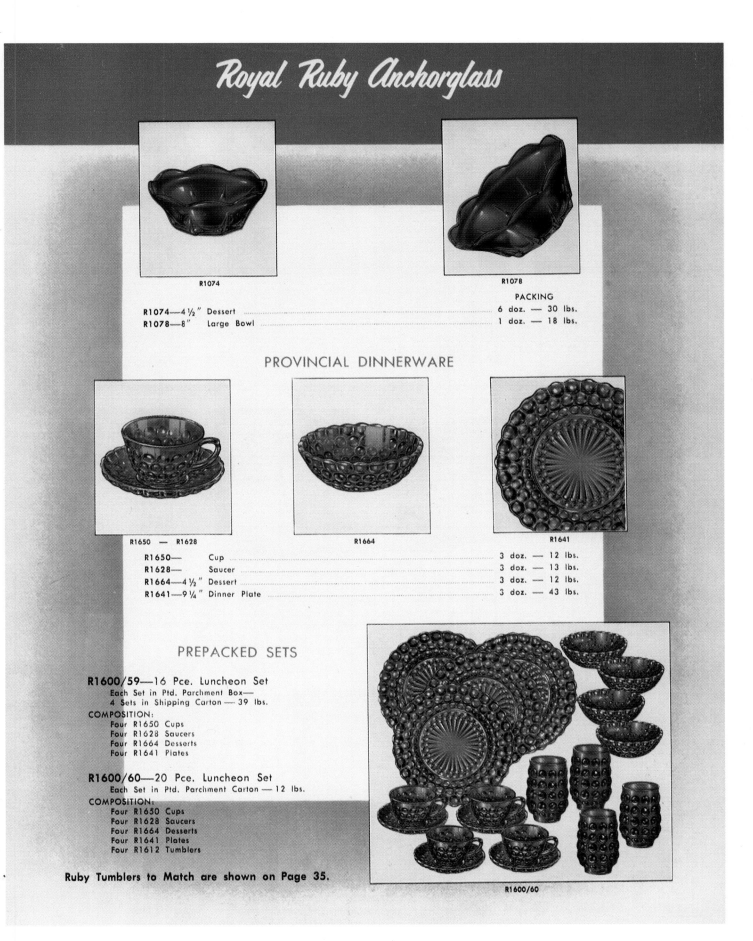

R1074

R1078

	PACKING	
R1074—4½″ Dessert	6 doz. —	30 lbs.
R1078—8″ Large Bowl	1 doz. —	18 lbs.

PROVINCIAL DINNERWARE

R1650 — R1628

R1664

R1641

R1650—	Cup	3 doz. —	12 lbs.
R1628—	Saucer	3 doz. —	13 lbs.
R1664—4½″	Dessert	3 doz. —	12 lbs.
R1641—9¼″	Dinner Plate	3 doz. —	43 lbs.

PREPACKED SETS

R1600/59—16 Pce. Luncheon Set
Each Set in Ptd. Parchment Box—
4 Sets in Shipping Carton — 39 lbs.
COMPOSITION:
    Four R1650 Cups
    Four R1628 Saucers
    Four R1664 Desserts
    Four R1641 Plates

R1600/60—20 Pce. Luncheon Set
Each Set in Ptd. Parchment Carton — 12 lbs.
COMPOSITION:
    Four R1650 Cups
    Four R1628 Saucers
    Four R1664 Desserts
    Four R1641 Plates
    Four R1612 Tumblers

Ruby Tumblers to Match are shown on Page 35.

R1600/60

R1600/55—9 Pce. Refreshment Set
Each Set in Printed Parchment Box,
4 Sets to Shipping Carton — 31 lbs.
COMPOSITION:
    Eight R1612 Tumblers
    One R1660 Pitcher

R1600/56—24 Pce. Hostess Service Set
Each Set in Printed Parchment
Carton — 12 lbs.
COMFOSITION:
    Eight R1606 Juice Glasses
    Eight R1612 Tumblers
    Eight R1616 Iced Teas

R1606

R1609

PACKING

R1606—6 oz. Fruit Juice .... 3 doz. — 10 lbs.
R1609—9 oz. Old Fashioned .... 3 doz. — 15 lbs.

See Page 21 for Luncheon Sets in Royal Ruby.

R1600/57—25 Pce. Refreshment Set
Each Set in Printed Parchment
Carton — 16 lbs.
COMPOSITION:
    Eight R1606 Juice Glasses
    Eight R1612 Tumblers
    Eight R1616 Iced Teas
    One R1660 Pitcher

R1600/58—24 Pce. Hostess Service Set
Each Set in Printed Parchment
Carton — 12 lbs.
COMPOSITION:
    Six R1606 Juice Glasses
    Six R1609 Old Fashioneds
    Six R1612 Tumblers
    Six R1616 Iced Teas

R1612 — R1616

R1660

R1612—12 oz. Tumbler .... 3 doz. — 18 lbs.
R1616—16 oz. Iced Tea .... 3 doz. — 22 lbs.
R1660—64 oz. Ice Lip Pitcher .... ½ doz. — 17 lbs.

ROLY POLY TUMBLERS

R3600/455—18 Pce. Hostess Service Set
Each Set in Printed Parchment
Carton — 6 lbs.
COMPOSITION:
    Six R3653 Juice Glasses
    Six R3651 Tumblers
    Six R3658 Iced Teas

R3653 — R3651

R3658

R3653— 5 oz. Fruit Juice .... 6 doz. — 16 lbs.
R3651— 9 oz. Table Tumbler .... 6 doz. — 24 lbs.
R3658—13 oz. Iced Tea .... 6 doz. — 30 lbs.

See Page 67 for Royal Ruby Ash Trays and Page 69 for Royal Ruby Vases.

FOREST GREEN Anchorglass®
Dinnerware

E1600/46—22 PCE. LUNCHEON SET
Each Set in Gift Ctn., 4 Sets to Shipping Ctn.—50 lbs.
COMPOSITION:

Four E1650 Cups	Four E336 Goblets
Four E1628 Saucers	One E1653 Sugar
Four E1665 Cereals	One E1654 Creamer
Four E1641 Dinner Plates	

E1600/45—18 PCE. LUNCHEON SET
Each Set in Gift Ctn., 4 Sets
to Shipping Ctn.—42 lbs.
COMPOSITION:

Four E1650 Cups   Four E1641-9¼" Plates
Four E1628 Saucers   One E1653 Sugar
Four E1665 Cereals   One E1654 Creamer

E1600/47—30 PCE. LUNCHEON SET
Each Set in Shipping Ctn.—22 lbs.
COMPOSITION:

Four E1650 Cups   Four E336 Goblets
Four E1628 Saucers   Four E333 Sherbets
Four E1665 Cereals   One E1653 Sugar
Four E1630-6⅜" Plates   One E1654 Creamer
Four E1641-9¼" Plates

FOREST GREEN AND CRYSTAL STEMWARE

E336—9½ OZ. GOBLET
Pkd. 3 doz.—17 lbs.

E335—5½ OZ. F. JUICE
Pkd. 3 doz.—10 lbs.

E334—4½ OZ. COCKTAIL
Pkd. 3 doz.—9 lbs.

E333—6 OZ. SHERBET
Pkd. 3 doz.—16 lbs.

E300/174—8 PCE. GOBLET SET
8 Pieces in Gift Ctn.—
6 Sets to Shipping Ctn.—26 lbs.
COMP.: Eight E336 Goblets

E300/175—8 PCE. JUICE SET
8 Pieces in Gift Ctn.—
6 Sets to Shipping Ctn.—15 lbs.
COMP.: Eight E335 Juice Glasses

E300/176—8 PCE. COCKTAIL SET
8 Pieces in Gift Ctn.—
6 Sets to Shipping Ctn.—15 lbs.
COMP.: Eight E334 Cocktails

E300/177—8 PCE. SHERBET SET
8 Pieces in Gift Ctn.—
6 Sets to Shipping Ctn.—24 lbs.
COMP.: Eight E333 Sherbets

E1650—8 OZ. CUP
Pkd. 6 doz.—22 lbs.

E1628—5¾" SAUCER
Pkd. 6 doz.—24 lbs.

E1665—5¼" CEREAL
Pkd. 6 doz.—35 lbs.

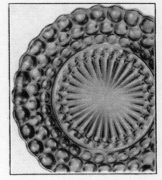

E1630—6⅝" PIE OR
SALAD PLATE
Pkd. 6 doz.—38 lbs.

E1641—9¼" DINNER
PLATE
Pkd. 3 doz.—38 lbs.

E1653—FOOTED
SUGAR
Pkd. 3 doz.—18 lbs.

E1654—FOOTED
CREAMER
Pkd. 3 doz.—18 lbs.

CABOCHON A.H.HEISEY & COMPANY, 1950-1957

Colors: Amber, crystal and Dawn.

In the first of three printings of the first edition of this book, there was a pattern shot mistake. A Lodestar Dawn colored sugar bowl was placed below the large grouping instead of the Cabochon. If anyone besides Dick Spencer noticed, they did not bother to write me about it. This error was spotted at the first glass show I took the book to which just happened to be the Belleville, Illinois, show sponsored by a Heisey Glass Club! If you have that first printing flawed copy, you can hope that mistake will make it more valuable someday!

This 1950's Heisey pattern has received some notice outside the world of Heisey collectors after its introduction in this book. Although there are a few pieces found in the desirable Amber and Dawn, Cabochon is mostly found in crystal. Prices now are reasonable for this pattern that was made near the end of the Heisey company's closing in 1957. This listing is taken from a 1953 catalogue.

	Crystal		Crystal
Bon bon, 6¼", hndl.,		Relish, 9", three part, oblong #1951	20.00
(sides sloped w/squared hndl.) #1951	22.50	Relish, 9", three part, square #1951	17.50
Bottle, oil, w/#101 stopper #1951	27.50	Salt and pepper, square, w/#60 silver	
Bowl, 4½", dessert #1951	4.00	plated tops, pr. #1951	12.50
Bowl, 5", dessert #1951	5.00	Saucer #1951	1.50
Bowl, 7", cereal #1951	6.00	Sherbet, 6 oz. #1951 (pressed)	4.00
Bowl, 13", floral or salad #1951	17.50	Sherbet, 6 oz. #6092 (blown)	4.00
Bowl, 13", gardenia		Stemware, 1 oz., cordial #6091	14.00
(low w/edge cupped irregularly) #1951	17.50	Stemware, 3 oz., oyster cocktail #6091	4.00
Butter dish, ¼ lb. #1951	25.00	Stemware, 3 oz., wine #6091	8.00
Cake salver, ftd. #1951	62.50	Stemware, 4 oz., cocktail #6091	4.00
Candle holder, 2 lite, ground bottom, pr. #1951	130.00	Stemware, 5½ oz., sherbet #6091	4.00
Candlette, 1 lite (like bowl), pr. #1951	35.00	Stemware, 10 oz., goblet #6091	8.00
Candy, 6¼", w/lid (bowl w/lid) #1951	30.00	Sugar, w/cover #1951	14.00
Cheese, 5¾", ftd., compote for cracker plate	17.50	Tidbit, 7½" (bowl w/sloped outsides) #1951	12.50
Cream #1951	9.00	Tray, 9", for cream and sugar #1951	37.50
Creamer, cereal, 12 oz. #1951	27.50	Tumbler, 5 oz. #1951 (pressed)	6.00
Cup #1951	6.00	Tumbler, 5 oz., juice, flat bottomed #6092 (blown)	6.00
Jelly, 6", hndl., (sides and hndl. rounded) #1951	22.50	Tumbler, 5 oz., juice, ftd. #6091	6.00
Mayonnaise, 3 pc. (plate, bowl, ladle) #1951	25.00	Tumbler, 10 oz., beverage #6092 (blown)	7.50
Mint, 5¾", ftd., (sides slanted) #1951	22.50	Tumbler, 10 oz., tumbler #6092 (blown)	7.50
Pickle tray, 8½" #1951	20.00	Tumbler, 12 oz. #1951 (pressed)	12.00
Plate, 8", salad #1951	6.00	Tumbler, 12 oz., ice tea #6092 (blown)	12.00
Plate, 13", center hndl. #1951	37.50	Tumbler, 12 oz., ice tea, ftd. #6091	7.50
Plate, 14", cracker w/center ring #1951	17.50	Tumbler, 14 oz., soda #6092 (blown)	10.00
Plate, 14", party (edge cupped irregularly) #1951	17.50	Vase, 3½", flared #1951	17.50
Plate, 14", sandwich #1951	17.50		

CAPRI "SEASHELL," "SWIRL COLONIAL," "COLONIAL." "ALPINE," HAZEL WARE,
DIVISION OF CONTINENTAL CAN, 1960's

Color: Azure blue.

I am now certain that "Capri" refers to the blue color of this ware rather than a pattern. However, for now, the various patterns are being lumped under the color name "Capri." As with Hazel Ware's purple color named Moroccan Amethyst, Capri labels have been found on numerous different patterns. (Hazel Ware, by the way, had previously been called Hazel Atlas before being bought out by Continental Can.) I still have seen no catalogue listings showing Capri pieces, but many labeled pieces and boxed sets are being found that say **CAPRI**. See the Seashell Snack Set pictured on the top of page 25 as an example. Evidently "Seashell" was the pattern name of the swirled ware since other colors also say "Seashell." You will find swirled "Seashell" bowls in green, amber and white! They are usually priced reasonably in these colors; I suspect that they are later productions made to go with the 1970's Avocado and Harvest Gold colors prevalent then.

Punch sets in "Seashell" (swirled design) are being found in crystal, white and amethyst. So far, a Capri punch set has not been reported, but its existence would not surprise me. Sets of crystal have been found with two different names: Swirl Colonial Crystal Punch Set and Colonial Crystal Punch Set. These are selling in the $20.00 to $25.00 range, but demand has been slow for crystal. You can see the Moroccan Amethyst set with white on the bottom of page 129. This set is called "Alpine" and will be discussed under Moroccan Amethyst.

As I suggested in the first book, Capri is now approaching thirty years since production, with more and more pieces finding their way out of homes through garage, tag and estate sales. It seems to take about twenty to thirty years to create a secondary market of a limited production pattern. If a pattern were widely distributed, then it does not take as long for people to start looking for items to complete sets that were never finished when the pattern was being made. That is happening! I just found a new style tumbler only a few days before my December photography session for this book. You can see examples of this squared foot tumbler with a swirled design on the bottom of page 24. The only examples I have measured are 2¾", 4 oz. and 3¹⁄₁₆", 6 oz, but I am including some readers' measurements.

On the top of page 24 you can see the Capri rounded style with dotted designs that Kathryn Forest of Alabama so graciously brought to me at the Peach State show last year. Note the dots on these pieces. (I said "circular dots" last time and received a letter reminding me that "circular dots" is redundant!) I have shown a crystal creamer and sugar with lid in the same pattern since the lid to the blue sugar and creamer has eluded me.

See the round ash tray at the bottom of page 25. It is an advertisement for a funeral home in Kentucky. I had to have that for the book! Was it coincidence that a funeral home found ash trays an appropriate stimulus for business?

I would also like to thank all readers who have furnished additional listings for this book. Capri is a color that has caught your eye. Keep looking! I am positive there are more pieces awaiting discovery!

	Blue		Blue
Ash tray, 3¼", triangular	6.00	Plate, 7⅛", round, salad, swirled sq bottom	7.00
Ash tray, 3¼", round	6.00	Plate, 7¼", salad, octagonal	7.50
Ash tray, 6⅞", triangular	12.00	Plate, 9½", round, snack w/cup rest	8.50
Bowl, 4¾", octagonal	7.50	Plate, 9¾", dinner, octagonal	10.00
Bowl, 4¾", swirled	8.00	Plate, 9⅞", dinner, round, "Hobnails"	10.00
Bowl, 4⅞", round, "Dots"	7.00	Plate, 10", snack, fan shaped w/cup rest	8.50
Bowl, 5⅜", salad, round, "Hobnails"	7.50	Saucer, 6", round, "Hobnails"	2.00
Bowl, 5⅝, swirled, sq. bottom	8.50	Saucer, octagonal	2.00
Bowl, 5¾", square, deep	10.00	Stem, 4½", sherbet	7.50
Bowl, 6", round, "Dots"	9.00	Stem, 5½", water	10.00
Bowl, 6", round, sq bottom	8.00	Sugar w/lid, round	12.50
Bowl, 7¾", oval	16.00	Tid bit, 3 tier	
Bowl, 7¾", rectangular	16.00	(round 9⅞" plate, 7⅛" plate, 6" saucer)	22.50
Bowl, 8¾", swirled	18.00	Tumbler, 2¾", 4oz., swirled, sq. bottom	7.00
Bowl, 9⅛" x 3" high	22.00	Tumbler, 3", 4oz., fruit "Dots"	7.00
Bowl, 9½" x 2⅞" high	20.00	Tumbler, 3", 5oz., pentagonal bottom	7.00
Bowl, 9½" oval 1½" high	9.00	Tumbler, 3¹⁄₁₆", swirled or plain, sq. bottom	8.00
Bowl, 10¾", salad	25.00	Tumbler, 3⅛", 5oz., pentagonal	8.00
Candy jar, w/cover, ftd.	30.00	Tumbler, 3¼", 8oz., old fashioned, "Dots"	7.50
Chip and dip, 2 swirled bowls		Tumbler, 3⅝", 3oz., "Dots"	7.00
(8¾" and 4¾" on metal rack)	30.00	Tumbler, 4¼", 9oz., swirled, sq. bottom	7.50
Creamer, round	8.00	Tumbler, 4¼", 9oz., water, pentagonal bottom	7.50
Cup, octagonal	6.00	Tumbler, 5", 12oz., swirled, sq. bottom	9.00
Cup, round, "Hobnails"	6.00	Tumbler, 5", 12oz., tea, pentagonal bottom	9.00
Cup, round, swirled	6.00	Tumbler, 6", 10oz., "Dots"	10.00
Plate, 5¾", bread and butter, octagonal	5.00	Vase, 8½", ruffled	35.00
Plate, 7", salad, round, swirled, sq. bottom	7.00		

Please refer to Foreword for pricing information

24

CASCADE - 4000 LINE CAMBRIDGE GLASS COMPANY, 1950's

Colors: Crystal, Emerald Green, Mandarin Gold and Milk White.

Cascade is one of the later made patterns of Cambridge that is just now being noticed by collectors. Observe that several of the pieces had more than one use. The 8" ash tray serves not only in that capacity, but is also the punch bowl base when it is turned over. Then, too, it rests atop the 21" plate to become a buffet set. Said plate's versatility is shown again as it becomes the punch bowl liner in the punch set. It is smart marketing!

Two water goblets are shown side by side on the bottom of page 28. Notice the stems on these. There are two distinct styles since one is turned upside down from the other. I do not know which is the harder to find. It seems the only difficulty to concern you in obtaining stemware.

	Crystal	Green	Yellow		Crystal	Green	Yellow
Ash tray, 4½"	6.00			Plate, 6½", bread & butter	5.50		
Ash tray, 6"	10.00			Plate, 8½", salad	7.50		
Ash tray, 8"	20.00			Plate, 8", 2 hdld., ftd. bonbon	12.50		
Bowl, 4½", fruit	7.00			Plate, 11½", 4 ftd.	17.50		
Bowl, 6½", relish	12.00			Plate, 14", 4 ftd. torte	22.50		
Bowl, 6½", relish, 2 pt.	12.00			Plate, 21"	45.00		
Bowl, 6", 4 ftd. bonbon	10.00			Punch base (same as 8" ash tray)	20.00		
Bowl, 7", 2 hdld., ftd., bonbon	12.50			Punch bowl liner, 21"	45.00		
Bowl, 10", 3 pt., celery	17.50			Punch bowl, 15"	110.00		
Bowl, 10", 4 ftd., flared	20.00			Punch cup	7.50		
Bowl, 10½", 4 ftd., shallow	22.50			Saucer	2.50		
Bowl, 12", 4 ftd., oval	25.00			Shaker, pr.	18.00		
Bowl, 12½", 4 ftd., flared	27.50			Stem, cocktail	10.00		
Bowl, 13", 4 ftd., shallow	27.50			Stem, sherbet	9.00		
Buffet set (21" plate w/8" ash tray)	65.00			Stem, water goblet	12.50		
Candlestick, 5"	15.00	25.00	25.00	Sugar	8.00	17.00	17.00
Candlestick, 6", 2 lite	22.50			Tumbler, 5 oz., flat	9.00		
Candy box, w/cover	35.00	55.00	55.00	Tumbler, 5 oz., ftd.	9.00		
Cigarette box w/cover	22.50			Tumbler, 12 oz., ftd.	12.00		
Comport, 5½"	17.50			Tumbler, 12 oz., flat	11.00		
Creamer	8.50	17.50	17.50	*Vase 9½"	30.00	60.00	60.00
Cup	8.00			Vase, 9½", oval	32.50		
Ice tub, tab hdld.	32.50						
Mayonnaise spoon	7.50			**Milk White $37.50**			
Mayonnaise, w/liner	17.50	45.00	45.00				

Please refer to Foreword for pricing information

Footed Bowl

Mayonnaise Set

Ash Tray

CASCADE
By CAMBRIDGE

Like a stream of pure light tumbling rhythmically into sun-splashed pools, Cascade brings you one of the most fascinating, brilliant *new* crystal designs to be seen in years. It is hand-made *modern* crystal in a variety of pieces . . . substantial, practical . . . ideal for formal or informal occasions.

You will fall in love with Cascade for yourself and willingly share its beauty in gifts to others. Be sure to see this fine American crystal now . . . at good stores, priced moderately.

THE CAMBRIDGE GLASS COMPANY • CAMBRIDGE, OHIO

CENTURY, LINE #2630, FOSTORIA GLASS COMPANY

Color: Crystal.

Prices for stemware and serving pieces in Century continue to increase. Wines, water goblets and footed iced teas have all increased due to demand more than scarcity. Nationally, prices are beginning to stabilize. However, prices for Elegant glassware in general are more reasonable in the western states than are the prices for Depression glassware. Dealers are now having a difficult time stocking basic patterns in Depression ware, and serving pieces in most patterns are fetching whatever the market will bear. It is very possible that such scarcity will occur twenty years hence in the 40's, 50's and 60's glassware.

As with most of Fostoria's patterns, there are two sizes of dinner plates. The 10½" dinner plate is the harder to find. They were priced higher originally, and many people did without the larger plates. Prices below are for mint (not scratched or worn) plates. Any pattern with plain centered plates needs to be examined carefully for use marks. It is very difficult to cut tough meat without leaving some evidence that you did!

The ice bucket has a metal handle and tabs for the handle to attach as shown in the bottom photograph. The 8½" oval vase is shaped like the ice bucket but without the "tabs." This vase is shown in upper right of the top picture.

A 7" candy is shown in the bottom photo. The 6" preserve is not as deep and is shorter; so do not confuse these. Remember, Century was the line used for many of Fostoria's late etched patterns, just as Fairfax was used for many of the earlier patterns.

	Crystal		Crystal
Ash tray, 2¾"	10.00	Pitcher, 7⅛", 48 oz.	95.00
Basket, 10¼" x 6½", wicker hndl.	67.50	Plate, 6½", bread/butter	6.00
Bowl, 4½", hndl.	12.00	Plate, 7½", salad	8.00
Bowl, 5", fruit	13.50	Plate, 7½", crescent salad	35.00
Bowl, 6", cereal	22.50	Plate, 8", party, w/indent for cup	22.50
Bowl, 6¼", snack, ftd.	13.00	Plate, 8½", luncheon	10.00
Bowl, 7⅛", 3 ftd., triangular	15.00	Plate, 9½", small dinner	22.50
Bowl, 7¼", bonbon, 3 ftd.	20.00	Plate, 10", hndl., cake	20.00
Bowl, 8", flared	25.00	Plate, 10½", dinner	30.00
Bowl, 8½", salad	25.00	Plate, 14", torte	30.00
Bowl, 9", lily pond	30.00	Platter, 12"	47.50
Bowl, 9½", hndl., serving bowl	27.50	Preserve, w/cover, 6"	35.00
Bowl, 9½", oval, serving bowl	32.50	Relish, 7⅜", 2 part	15.00
Bowl, 10", oval, hndl.	30.00	Relish, 11⅛", 3 part	22.50
Bowl, 10½", salad	27.50	Salt and pepper, 2⅜", (individual), pr.	15.00
Bowl, 10¾", ftd., flared	30.00	Salt and pepper, 3⅛", pr.	20.00
Bowl, 11, ftd., rolled edge	40.00	Salver, 12¼", ftd. (like cake stand)	47.50
Bowl, 11¼", lily pond	32.50	Saucer	4.00
Bowl, 12", flared	32.50	Stem, 3½ oz., cocktail, 4⅛"	19.00
Butter, w/cover, ¼ lb.	35.00	Stem, 3½ oz., wine, 4½"	30.00
Candy, w/cover, 7"	35.00	Stem, 4½ oz., oyster cocktail, 3¾"	20.00
Candlestick, 4½"	17.50	Stem, 5½ oz., sherbet, 4½"	12.00
Candlestick, 7", double	30.00	Stem, 10 oz., goblet, 5¾"	22.50
Candlestick, 7¾", triple	40.00	Sugar, 4", ftd.	9.00
Comport, 2¾", cheese	15.00	Sugar, individual	9.00
Comport, 4⅜"	20.00	Tid bit, 8⅛", 3 ftd., upturned edge	18.00
Cracker plate, 10¾"	30.00	Tid bit, 10¼", 2 tier, metal hndl.	25.00
Creamer, 4¼"	9.00	Tray, 4¼", for ind. salt/pepper	13.50
Creamer, individual	9.00	Tray, 7⅛", for ind. sugar/creamer	14.00
Cup, 6 oz., ftd.	15.00	Tray, 9⅛", hndl., utility	23.00
Ice Bucket	60.00	Tray, 9½", hndl., muffin	27.50
Mayonnaise, 3 pc.	30.00	Tray, 11½", center hndl.	30.00
Mayonnaise, 4 pc., div. w/2 ladles	35.00	Tumbler, 5 oz., ftd., juice, 4¾"	22.50
Mustard, w/spoon, cover	27.50	Tumbler, 12 oz., ftd., tea, 5⅞"	27.50
Oil, w/stopper, 5 oz.	45.00	Vase, 6", bud	18.00
Pickle, 8¾"	15.00	Vase, 7½", hndl.	67.50
Pitcher, 6⅛", 16 oz.	47.50	Vase, 8½", oval	65.00

Please refer to Foreword for pricing information

CHINTZ, (PLATE ETCHING #338), FOSTORIA GLASS COMPANY

Color: crystal.

At present, Chintz stemware continues to be abundant except for clarets. I just attended an antique show where two dealers had cordials for sale. The iced tea tumbler is the scarce footed tumbler. Serving pieces are elusive as anyone collecting this pattern will tell you.

Unlike many of the Fostoria patterns, there is only one size dinner plate in this pattern. You will have to settle for a 9½" plate. Scratched plates are the nemesis again, so choose your wares carefully. Prices below are for **mint** condition plates and not ones with "light" scratching!

The metal drip cut syrup was listed as Sani-cut in sales brochures. Evidently, this was not a "must-have" since they are so scarce today.

That oval divided bowl on the left in the bottom photograph is the divided sauce boat. That piece also comes undivided. The oval sauce boat liner came with both, but a brochure listed it as a tray instead of liner. Many pieces of Chintz pattern are found on the #2496 blank (known as Baroque). Novice collectors, that fleur-de-lis is the giveaway design for the Baroque blank.

Be on the lookout for dinner bells, finger bowls, salad dressing bottles, syrups and any of the vases. All these pieces are considered to be scarce in this pattern!

	Crystal		Crystal
Bell, dinner	110.00	Plate, #2496, 10½", hndl., cake	42.50
Bowl, #869, 4½", finger	37.50	Plate, #2496, 11", cracker	40.00
Bowl, #2496, 4⅝", tri-cornered	22.50	Plate, #2496, 14", upturned edge	50.00
Bowl, #2496, 5", fruit	27.50	Plate, #2496, 16", torte, plain edge	110.00
Bowl, #2496, 5", hndl.	25.00	Platter, #2496, 12"	90.00
Bowl, #2496, 7⅝", bon bon	32.50	Relish, #2496, 6", 2 part, square	32.00
Bowl, #2496, 8½", hndl.	50.00	Relish, #2496, 10" x 7½", 3 part	40.00
Bowl, #2496, 9½", vegetable	67.50	Relish, #2419, 5 part	40.00
Bowl, #2484, 10", hndl.	52.50	Salad dressing bottle, #2083, 6½"	300.00
Bowl, #2496, 10½", hndl.	65.00	Salt and pepper, #2496, 2¾", flat, pr.	87.50
Bowl, #2496, 11½", flared	60.00	Sauce boat, #2496, oval	70.00
Bowl, #6023, ftd.	37.50	Sauce boat, #2496, oval, divided	70.00
Candlestick, #2496, 3½", double	30.00	Sauce boat liner, #2496, oblong, 8"	30.00
Candlestick, #2496, 4"	17.50	Saucer, #2496	5.00
Candlestick, #2496, 5½"	30.00	Stem, #6026, 1 oz., cordial, 3⅞"	47.50
Candlestick, #2496, 6", triple	40.00	Stem, #6026, 4 oz., cocktail, 5"	26.00
Candlestick, #6023, double	35.00	Stem, #6026, 4 oz., oyster cocktail, 3⅜"	27.50
Candy, w/cover, #2496, 3 part	115.00	Stem, #6026, 4½ oz., claret-wine, 5⅜"	40.00
Celery, #2496, 11"	35.00	Stem, #6026, 6 oz., low sherbet, 4⅜"	20.00
Comport, #2496, 3¼", cheese	25.00	Stem, #6026, 6 oz., saucer champagne, 5½"	21.00
Comport, #2496, 4¾"	32.50	Stem, #6026, 9 oz., water goblet, 7⅝"	32.00
Comport, #2496, 5½"	37.50	Sugar, #2496, 3½", ftd.	16.00
Creamer, #2496, 3¾", ftd.	17.00	Sugar, #2496½, individual	21.00
Creamer, #2496½, individual	22.50	Syrup, #2586, Sani-cut	350.00
Cup, #2496, ftd.	21.00	Tidbit, #2496, 8¼", 3 ftd., upturned edge	26.00
Ice bucket, #2496	127.50	Tray, #2496½, 6½", for ind. sugar/creamer	21.00
Jelly, w/cover, #2496, 7½"	82.00	Tray, #2375, 11", center hndl.	40.00
Mayonnaise, #2496½, 3 piece	57.50	Tumbler, #6026, 5 oz., juice, ftd.	26.00
Oil, w/stopper, #2496, 3½ oz.	97.50	Tumbler, #6026, 9 oz., water or low goblet	26.00
Pickle, #2496, 8"	32.00	Tumbler, #6026, 13 oz., tea, ftd.	32.00
Pitcher, #5000, 48 oz., ftd.	350.00	Vase, #4108, 5"	80.00
Plate, #2496, 6", bread/butter	10.00	Vase, #4128, 5"	80.00
Plate, #2496, 7½", salad	15.00	Vase, #4143, 6", ftd.	95.00
Plate, #2496, 8½", luncheon	21.00	Vase, #4143, 7½", ftd.	130.00
Plate, #2496, 9½", dinner	47.50		

"CHRISTMAS CANDY," NO. 624 INDIANA GLASS COMPANY, 1950's

Colors: Terrace Green and crystal.

"Christmas Candy" is another of Indiana's numbered lines (#624), and almost all the pieces I have bought over the years have come from my trips into Indiana. "Christmas Candy" may have been only regionally distributed. Dunkirk, the home of Indiana Glass, is not far from Indianapolis where I used to attend several Depression Glass shows each year.

The 9½" vegetable bowl first shown in the previous edition of this book created quite a stir among "Christmas Candy" collectors. It had been a long time since a new piece of this pattern had been found! You might expect that the newly discovered vegetable bowl **would** be found in Indiana and be brought to the Indianapolis Depression Glass show!

I omitted the crystal tidbit in the listing last time even though I had it pictured. Sorry. The bowl atop the tidbit measures 5¾". Crystal "Christmas Candy" has few collectors, but it is a pattern that can still be found at reasonable prices. Some of the pieces of teal are no longer "reasonably priced" as you can see below. (Of course, reasonable pricing is relative. Ten years from now, we may think these were *very* reasonable prices for these scarce items!)

Teal, or "Terrace Green" as it was named by the company, is the color everyone wants. Unfortunately, there is very little of this color found today. Usually, "Christmas Candy" is found in sets rather than a piece here and there. Any glassware made in the 1950's is often found in sets — having been carefully stored in someone's attic, garage or basement.

I will repeat the information found on a boxed set from the first book. On a 15-piece set was the following: "15 pc. Luncheon set (Terrace Green) To F W Newburger & Co. New Albany Ind Dept M 1346; From Pitman Dretzer Dunkirk Ind 4-3-52." This was valuable dated information because this color was attributed to much earlier production in other published information.

	Crystal	Teal
Bowl, 5¾"	4.00	
Bowl, 7⅜", soup	7.00	30.00
Bowl, 9½", vegetable		150.00
Creamer	9.00	20.00
Cup	5.00	19.00
Mayonnaise, w/ladle, liner	20.00	
Plate, 6", bread and butter	3.50	11.00
Plate, 8¼", luncheon	7.00	17.50
Plate, 9⅝", dinner	10.00	30.00
Plate, 11¼", sandwich	15.00	40.00
Saucer	2.00	7.00
Sugar	9.00	20.00
Tidbit, 2-tier	17.50	

COIN GLASS, LINE #1372, FOSTORIA GLASS COMPANY, 1958-1982

Colors: Amber, blue, crystal, green, Olive green and red.

Coin glass is rapidly becoming a hot collectible in today's markets. With that sentence I opened a can of worms in the first edition of this book. Even though I have had hundreds of letters thanking me for finally providing a price guide for Fostoria's Coin glass, I was sorry that I had included the pattern before the book was ever off the press. I included Coin because it was becoming an increasingly desirable collectible–so desirable, in fact, that Lancaster Colony, who now owns the Fostoria moulds, began remaking it! I don't mean moulding a few pieces but producing a whole line in many of the original colors! Needless to say, this has set the prices in disarray. The quandary I now have is how to handle it. **Know your dealer and remember, if the price sounds too good to be true, it probably is!**

First of all, several people are sand blasting or satinizing the non-frosted coins! That addresses only one small problem, but it needs to be pointed out before I repeat what I said in the first edition:

Coin glass is currently being made by Lancaster Colony who bought the Fostoria Company. The Coin pieces in production now do not have frosted coins! All prices below are for pieces that have frosted coins. I have heard it said that those pieces without frosted coins were sold only in the outlet stores. Okay, that may be true; but I know that I saw the frosted coin pieces in the outlet stores back in the late 1970's and early 1980's when I first started working on my Elegant Glassware of the Depression Era. I was trying to keep up with the American pattern issues that were being made then; so I made many trips to outlet stores in Cambridge, Ohio, and Wheeling, West Virginia, during that time. By the way, unfrosted pieces can still be frosted today with the right equipment.

Thankfully, the blue and green colors currently being manufactured are different shades than those originally made. I have photographed these new colors on the bottom of page 39 with the original colors shown in the photos at the top of that page.

The Olive Green is sometimes referred to as avocado, but Olive was the official name. The green that is most desired is often called "emerald" by collectors. This color is represented by the jelly and cruet set shown on page 39.

You will find some crystal with gold decorated coins. This sells for about double the price of normal crystal if the gold is not worn. It is almost impossible to sell with worn or faded gold.

Reports are that crystal tumblers and stems may be remade this year! Be aware of this possibility.

	Amber	Blue	Crystal	Green	Olive	Ruby
Ash tray, 5" #1372/123	17.50	25.00	18.00	30.00	17.50	22.50
Ash tray, 7½", center coin #1372/119	20.00		25.00	35.00		25.00
Ash tray, 7½", round #1372/114	25.00	40.00	25.00	45.00	30.00	20.00
Ash tray, 10" #1372/124	30.00	50.00	25.00	55.00	30.00	
Ash tray, oblong #1372/115	15.00	20.00	10.00	25.00	25.00	
Ash tray/cover, 3" #1372/110	20.00	25.00	25.00	30.00		
Bowl, 8", round #1372/179	30.00	50.00	25.00	70.00	25.00	45.00
Bowl, 8½", ftd. #1372/199	60.00	85.00	50.00	100.00	50.00	70.00
Bowl, 8½", ftd. w/cover #1372/212	100.00	150.00	85.00	175.00		
Bowl, 9", oval #1372/189	30.00	55.00	30.00	70.00	30.00	50.00
*Bowl, wedding w/cover #1372/162	70.00	90.00	55.00	125.00	55.00	85.00
Candle holder, 4½", pr. #1372/316	30.00	50.00	40.00	50.00	30.00	50.00
Candle holder, 8", pr. #1372/326	60.00		50.00		50.00	95.00
Candy box w/cover, 4⅛" #1372/354	30.00	60.00	30.00	75.00	30.00	60.00
*Candy jar w/cover, 6⁵⁄₁₆" #1372/347	25.00	50.00	25.00	75.00	25.00	50.00
*Cigarette box w/cover, 5¾" x 4½" #1372/374	50.00	75.00	40.00	100.00		
Cigarette holder w/ash tray cover #1372/372	50.00	75.00	45.00	90.00		
Cigarette urn, 3⅜", ftd. #1372/381	25.00	45.00	20.00	50.00	20.00	40.00
Condiment set, 4 pc. (tray, 2 shakers and cruet) #1372/737	210.00	270.00	130.00		205.00	
Condiment tray, 9⅝", #1372/738	60.00	75.00	40.00		75.00	
Creamer #1372/680	11.00	16.00	10.00	30.00	15.00	16.00
Cruet, 7 oz. w/stopper #1372/531	65.00	100.00	50.00	150.00	80.00	
*Decanter w/stopper, pint, 10³⁄₁₆" #1372/400	120.00	160.00	80.00	325.00	120.00	
Jelly #1372/448	17.50	25.00	15.00	35.00	15.00	25.00
Lamp chimney, coach or patio #1372/461	45.00	60.00	35.00			

*Gold coins double price of crystal.

Please refer to Foreword for pricing information

COIN GLASS #1372 (Cont.)

	Amber	Blue	Crystal	Green	Olive	Ruby
Lamp chimney, hndl., courting #1372/292	35.00	60.00				
Lamp, 9¾", hndl., courting, oil #1372/310	100.00	150.00				
Lamp, 10⅛", hndl., courting, electric #1372/311	100.00	150.00				
Lamp, 13½", coach, electric #1372/321	125.00	175.00	95.00			
Lamp, 13½", coach, oil #1372/320	125.00	175.00	95.00			
Lamp, 16⅝", patio, electric #1372/466	145.00	250.00	125.00			
Lamp, 16⅝", patio, oil #1372/459	145.00	250.00	125.00			
Nappy, 4½" #1372/495			18.00			
Nappy, 5⅜", w/hndl. #1372/499	20.00	30.00	15.00	40.00	18.00	30.00
Pitcher, 32 oz., 6⁵⁄₁₆" #1372/453	50.00	100.00	45.00	125.00	50.00	80.00
Plate, 8", #1372/550			20.00		20.00	40.00
Punch bowl base #1372/602			150.00			
Punch bowl, 14", 1½ gal., #1372/600			150.00			
Punch cup #1372/615			30.00			
Salver, ftd., 6½" tall #1372/630	110.00	150.00	90.00	250.00	115.00	
Shaker, 3¼", pr. w/chrome top #1372/652	30.00	45.00	25.00	90.00	30.00	45.00
Stem, 4", 5 oz. wine #1372/26			30.00		45.00	60.00
Stem, 5¼", 9 oz., sherbet, #1372/7			20.00		40.00	60.00
Stem, 10½ oz., goblet #1372/2			30.00		45.00	85.00
Sugar w/cover #1372/673	35.00	45.00	25.00	60.00	30.00	45.00
Tumbler, 3⅝", 9 oz. juice/old fashioned #1372/81			27.50			
Tumbler, 4¼", 9 oz. water, scotch & soda #1372/73			27.50			
Tumbler, 5⅛", 12 oz. ice tea/high ball #1372/64			35.00			
Tumbler, 5⅜", 10 oz. double old fashioned #1372/23			20.00			
Tumbler, 5³⁄₁₆", 14 oz. ice tea #1372/58			30.00		40.00	75.00
Urn, 12¾", ftd., w/cover #1372/829	80.00	125.00	75.00	200.00	80.00	100.00
Vase, 8", bud #1372/799	22.00	40.00	20.00	60.00	25.00	45.00
Vase, 10", ftd. #1372/818			45.00			

Please refer to Foreword for pricing information

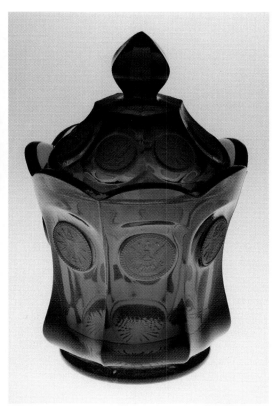

CROCHETED CRYSTAL IMPERIAL GLASS COMPANY, 1943-early 1950's

Color: Crystal.

Crocheted Crystal was made by Imperial exclusively for Sears, Roebuck and Company. The listing below is from the fall 1943 Sears catalogue. I was unable to locate any of the stemware in this pattern to show you what it looks like, so I will have to do that next time.

I first started looking at this pattern because the shapes and styles reminded me of Laced Edge, also made by Imperial. Some of the pieces I have pictured are not in the listing below, although they have all the characteristics of the pattern. In the top picture there is a four footed bowl that is not in that 1943 Sears list. I do not have all the Sears catalogues from this time period so there may be additional pieces not in my list. There are two styles of mayonnaise dishes pictured, but both seem to be Crocheted Crystal. In the bottom photograph the footed bowl and center handled bowl may not be correct, but they are great "go-with" items if not.

One of the more amazing things I met with in trying to buy this pattern was the variety of prices. No one seemed to know what it was, but they all had high prices because it was "pretty good glass" or "quality glass." At a show in Jacksonville, Florida, last year, I encountered the epergne shown in the bottom photograph. I inquired about the cost. The dealer informed me that it was unmarked Heisey and very rare. She could let it go for $175.00. I passed!

I have never understood how dealers can come up with an extraordinary price when they have no idea what they are pricing. You can guess based upon what you paid for it; but to tell someone what it is when you have no idea, is a big mistake!

	Crystal		Crystal
Basket, 6"	25.00	Narcissus bowl	35.00
Basket, 9"	35.00	Plate, 8", salad	7.50
Basket, 12"	55.00	Plate, 9½"	12.50
Bowl, 10½", salad	27.50	Plate, 13", salad bowl liner	20.00
Bowl, 11", console	27.50	Plate, 14"	20.00
Bowl, 12", console	30.00	Plate, 17"	35.00
Buffet set, 14" plate, ftd. sauce bowl, ladle	35.00	Punch bowl, 14"	65.00
Cake stand, 12", ftd.	40.00	Punch cup, open hdld.	5.00
Candleholder, 4½", 2-lite	17.50	Relish, 11½", 3 pt.	25.00
Celery, 10", oval	22.50	Stem, 4½", 3½ oz., cocktail	12.50
Cheese & cracker, 12" plate, ftd. dish	35.00	Stem, 5½", 4½ oz., wine	17.50
Creamer	12.50	Stem, 5", 6 oz., sherbet	10.00
Epergne, 11", ftd. bowl, center vase	125.00	Stem, 7⅛", 9 oz., water goblet	14.00
Hors d'oeuvre dish, 10½", 4 pt., round	30.00	Sugar	12.50
Lamp, 11", hurricane	30.00	Tumbler, 6", 6 oz., ftd. fruit juice	8.50
Mayonnaise bowl, 5¼"	12.50	Tumbler, 7⅛", 12 oz., ftd. iced tea	15.00
Mayonnaise ladle	5.00	Vase, 8"	17.50
Mayonnaise plate, 7½"	7.50		

"DAISY," NUMBER 620 INDIANA GLASS COMPANY

Colors: Crystal, 1933-40; fired-on red, late 30's; amber, 1940's; dark green and milk glass, 1960's, 1970's, 1980's.

"Daisy" is one of the few patterns that fit both my 1930's and 1950's glassware books; so a decision had to be made as to placement. Since more collectors search for the amber or green "Daisy," I decided that it best fit this book instead of *The Collector's Encyclopedia of Depression Glass*. Know that the crystal was made in 1930's, but there are few collectors of that today.

Avocado colored "Daisy" was marketed by Indiana as "Heritage" in the 1960's through 1980's and not under the name "Daisy" or No. 620 as it was when it was first produced in the late 1930's. I mention this because Federal Glass Company also made a "Heritage" pattern that is rare in green. Federal's green is the brighter, normally found Depression Glass color and not the avocado colored green shown here.

The pattern shot below shows an indented grill plate, which holds the cream soup and not the cup. The bottom of the cream soup fits it exactly, while the cup bottom is too small for the ring. The amber indented grill plate probably belongs in the hard to find category, but few collectors search for grill plates; so there is an adequate supply for the demand. I omitted the regular grill plate last time; I have added that to the listing.

Speaking of amber "Daisy," I have found that it is one of the few amber colored patterns that continue to escalate in price. Other amber patterns have had ups and downs, but "Daisy" prices have always steadily increased. Besides the indented grill plate, the 12 oz. footed tea, relish dish, 9⅜" berry and cereal bowls are all scarce at this time; not rare — but scarce!

There are a few pieces of red fired-on "Daisy" being found. A reader's letter last year said that her family had a red set that was purchased in 1935. So, that helps date this production. There is a pitcher in a fired-on red being found with the No. 618 tumblers. This pitcher does not belong to either pattern per se, but was sold with both of these Indiana patterns. Thus, it's a legitimate "go-with" pitcher.

	Crystal	Green	Red, Amber
Bowl, 4½", berry	4.50	6.00	9.00
Bowl, 4½", cream soup	4.50	6.00	12.00
Bowl, 6", cereal	10.00	12.00	28.00
Bowl, 7⅜", deep berry	7.50	9.00	15.00
Bowl, 9⅜", deep berry	13.00	16.00	30.00
Bowl, 10", oval vegetable	9.50	11.00	16.00
Creamer, footed	5.50	5.00	8.00
Cup	4.00	4.00	6.00
Plate, 6", sherbet	2.00	2.00	3.00
Plate, 7⅜", salad	3.50	3.50	7.00
Plate, 8⅜", luncheon	4.00	4.50	6.00
Plate, 10⅜", grill	5.50	7.50	10.00
Plate, 9⅜", dinner	5.50	6.50	9.00
Plate, 10⅜", grill w/indent for cream soup		13.50	20.00
Plate, 11½", cake or sandwich	6.50	7.50	13.00
Platter, 10¾"	7.50	8.50	15.00
Relish dish, 8⅜", 3 part	12.00		30.00
Saucer	1.50	1.50	2.00
Sherbet, footed	5.00	5.50	9.00
Sugar, footed	5.50	5.00	8.00
Tumbler, 9 oz., footed	9.50	9.50	18.00
Tumbler, 12 oz., footed	19.00	20.00	35.00

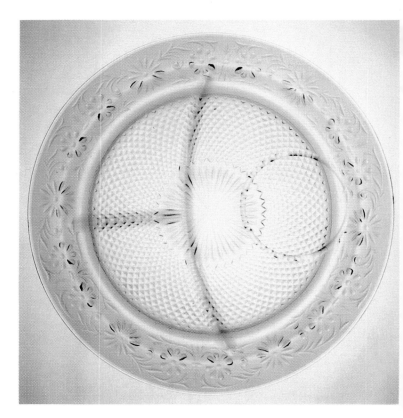

DEWDROP JEANNETTE GLASS COMPANY, 1953-1956

Color: Crystal.

Dewdrop is one of those patterns that you either love or hate. There does not seem to be any middle ground. The butter dish does have a bottom, but I could not find one to place with the top for this photography session. I did finally find one, but it will have to wait until the next book to make its appearance.

Many collectors are buying the lazy susan in this pattern to get the missing ball bearings for their Shell Pink lazy susan. These ball bearings are interchangeable. Note the original gift box shown with the lazy susan. A similar box in pink or blue was used for the lazy susan in Shell Pink.

I have included a photo of the iced tea tumbler since it was omitted before. The snack sets were sold as TV snack trays in sets of four. I have seen several boxed sets of these in my travels.

Dewdrop will not break your bank account now, so buy it. Someday you will not be sorry!

	Crystal
Bowl, 4¾"	4.00
Bowl, 8½"	11.00
Bowl, 10⅜"	16.50
Butter, w/cover	27.50
Candy dish, w/cover, 7", round	18.00
Creamer	8.00
Cup, punch or snack	4.00
Pitcher, ½ gallon	25.00
Plate, 11½"	16.00
Plate, snack, w/indent for cup	4.00
Punch bowl base	9.00
Punch bowl, 6 qt.	24.00
Relish, leaf shape w/hndl.	8.00
Sugar, w/cover	13.00
Tray, 13", lazy susan	20.00
Tumbler, 9 oz., water	10.00
Tumbler, 15 oz., iced tea	15.00

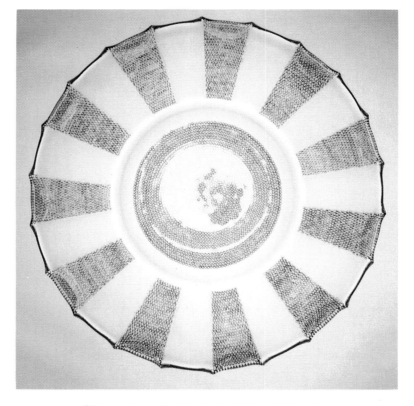

Please refer to Foreword for pricing information

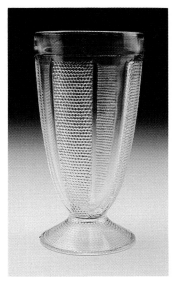

EMERALD CREST FENTON ART GLASS COMPANY, 1949-1955

Color: White with green edge.

Thanks for all the letters I received praising the addition of Fenton patterns in this book. I appreciate the time and help I have had obtaining accurate price listings for Emerald Crest and Silver Crest. I had intended to include Aqua Crest in this book, but the collector whose glass I was to use got divorced and moved to Arizona; so that will have to wait for another collector to volunteer their glass to photograph!

Emerald Crest, introduced in 1949, was listed in Fenton catalogues until January 1955. That means production was finished at least by the end of 1955. This popular line followed the Aqua Crest (blue trimmed), started in 1941, and Silver Crest (crystal trimmed) started in 1943. Prices for Aqua Crest fall between that of Emerald Crest and Silver Crest (that is priced on pages 176 and 178).

You may notice that there are two different sized tidbit bowls. One tidbit is made from the soup and 8½" bowl while the other is made from the 8½" and 10" bowls. Most mayonnaise sets are found with crystal spoons, but a green spoon was made. It is rarely found.

Some pieces of Emerald Crest have two different line numbers on them. Originally, this line was #680, and all pieces carried that designation. In July, 1952 Fenton began issuing a "Ware Number" for each piece. That is why you see two separate numbers for the different sized plates.

	White w/Green		White w/Green
Basket, 5" #7236	75.00	Mayonnaise set, 3 pc. w/gr. ladle #7203	75.00
Basket, 7" #7237	95.00	Mustard, w/lid and spoon	77.50
Bowl, 5", finger or deep dessert #7221	18.00	Oil bottle, w/green stopper #680, #7269	85.00
Bowl, 5½", soup #680, #7230	36.00	Pitcher, 6" hndl., beaded melon #7116	52.50
Bowl, 8½", flared #680	40.00	Plate, 5½" #680, #7218	15.00
Bowl, 9½" #682	57.50	Plate, 6½" #680, #7219	16.00
Bowl, 10" salad #7220	75.00	Plate, 8½" #680, #7217	32.50
Bowl, dessert, shallow #7222	19.00	Plate, 10" #680, #7210	38.00
Bowl, ftd., tall, square #7330	75.00	Plate, 12" #680, #7212	47.50
Cake plate, 13" high ftd. #680, #7213	77.50	Plate, 12" #682	47.50
Cake plate, low ftd. #5813	67.50	Plate, 16", torte #7216	62.00
Candle holder, flat saucer base, pr. #680	72.00	Saucer #7208	13.00
Comport, 6", ftd., flared #206	37.50	Sherbet, ftd. #7226	22.50
Comport, ftd., double crimped	37.50	Sugar, clear reeded hndls. #7231	36.00
Creamer, clear reeded hndls. #7231	42.50	Tidbit, 2 tier bowls, 5½" & 8½"	65.00
Cup #7208	35.00	Tidbit, 2 tier bowls, 8½" & 10"	85.00
Flower pot w/attached saucer #7299	67.50	Tidbit, 2 tier plates #7297	57.50
Mayonnaise bowl, #7203	32.50	Tidbit, 3 tier plates #7298	77.50
Mayonnaise ladle, crystal #7203	5.00	Vase, 4½", fan #36, #7355	23.00
Mayonnaise ladle, green, #7203	32.50	Vase, 6¼", fan #36, #7357	27.50
Mayonnaise liner, #7203	11.00	Vase, 8", bulbous base #186	60.00
Mayonnaise set, 3 pc. w/crys. ladle #7203	55.00		

ENGLISH HOBNAIL Line No. 555 WESTMORELAND GLASS COMPANY, 1920's-1983

Colors: Amber, crystal and crystal with various color treatments.

English Hobnail has been in my Depression era book since 1972; but crystal and amber English Hobnail pattern were made until Westmoreland closed in 1983. Thus, I am pricing amber and crystal in this book. Even though crystal with amber or black feet and some shades of amber were made before 1940, pricing is fairly consistent for all these colors that basically fit into the time frame of this book. The milk glass was made very late. You can double the price listed for any fruit decorated milk glass. Ruby flashed is difficult to sell at regular crystal prices.

The icer shown on the right back next to the comport (sweetmeat) on the top of page 49 is not in any of the catalogue listings I have. There were eight of these in a mall in Chattanooga, Tennessee, but I could only buy one for photography since the price was prohibitive to buy them all for resale. In the year since I purchased the one, the other seven are still there if that gives you a hint. Sometimes rarely found items do not sell because the right collector does not come along; and sometimes they do not sell because there are few collectors of that pattern or color!

	Amber/Crystal		Amber/Crystal		Amber/Crystal
Ash tray, 3"	5.00	Bowl, 11", bell	30.00	Cup, demitasse	15.00
Ash tray, 4½"	7.00	Bowl, 11", rolled edge	27.50	Decanter, 20 oz.	45.00
Ash tray, 4½", sq.	7.50	Bowl, 12", celery	17.50	Egg cup	10.00
Basket, 5", hdld.	15.00	Bowl, 12", flange or console	27.50	Hat, high	15.00
Basket, 6", tall, hdld.	35.00	Bowl, 12", flared	27.50	Hat, low	12.50
Bon bon, 6½", hdld.	12.50	Bowl, 12", oval crimped	32.50	Ice tub, 4"	17.50
Bottle, toilet, 5 oz.	17.50	Bowl, cream soup	10.00	Ice tub, 5½"	35.00
Bowl, 4", rose	15.00	Candelabra, 2-lite	17.50	Icer, sq. base,	
Bowl, 4½", finger	7.50	Candlestick, 3½", rnd. base	8.00	w/patterned insert	40.00
Bowl, 4½", round nappy	7.00	Candlestick, 5½", sq. base	15.00	Lamp, 6½", electric	30.00
Bowl, 4½", sq. ftd., finger	9.00	Candlestick, 9", rnd. base	22.50	Lamp, 9½", electric	40.00
Bowl, 4½", sq. nappy	7.00	Candy dish, 3 ftd.	30.00	Lamp, candlestick	
Bowl, 5", round nappy	9.50	Candy, ½ lb. and cover,		(several types)	30.00
Bowl, 5½", bell nappy	11.50	cone shaped	22.50	Lampshade, 17"	150.00
Bowl, 6", crimped dish	12.50	Chandelier, 17" shade		Marmalade w/cover	15.00
Bowl, 6", rose	17.50	w/200+ prisms	395.00	Mayonnaise, 6"	10.00
Bowl, 6", round nappy	10.00	Cheese w/cover, 6"	32.50	Mustard, sq. ftd., w/lid	15.00
Bowl, 6", sq. nappy	10.00	Cheese w/cover, 8¾"	47.50	Nut, individual, ftd.	6.00
Bowl, 6½", grapefruit	11.00	Cigarette box and cover,		Oil bottle, 2 oz., hdld.	20.00
Bowl, 6½", round nappy	12.00	4½"x2½"	17.50	Oil bottle, 6 oz., hdld.	30.00
Bowl, 6½", sq. nappy	12.50	Cigarette jar w/cover, rnd.	12.50	Oil-vinegar combination, 6 oz.	37.50
Bowl, 7", 6 pt.	15.00	Cigarette lighter		Parfait, rnd. ftd.	15.00
Bowl, 7", oblong spoon	17.50	(milk glass only)	10.00	Pitcher, 23 oz., rounded	45.00
Bowl, 7", preserve	13.50	Coaster, 3"	5.00	Pitcher, 32 oz., straight side	50.00
Bowl, 7", round nappy	13.00	Compote, 5", round, rnd. ftd.	12.00	Pitcher, 38 oz., rounded	60.00
Bowl, 7½", bell nappy	14.00	Compote, 5", sq. ftd., round	12.50	Pitcher, 60 oz., rounded	65.00
Bowl, 8", 6 pt.	22.50	Compote, 5½", ball stem,		Pitcher, 64 oz., straight side	75.00
Bowl, 8", cupped, nappy	20.00	sweetmeat	25.00	Plate, 5½", rnd.	4.50
Bowl, 8", ftd.	25.00	Compote, 5½", bell	14.00	Plate, 6", sq.	5.00
Bowl, 8", hexagonal ftd.,		Compote, 5½", sq. ftd., bell	15.00	Plate, 6", sq. finger bowl liner	5.00
2-hdld.	35.00	Compote, 6", honey, rnd. ftd.	15.00	Plate, 6½", depressed center, rnd.	6.00
Bowl, 8", pickle	12.50	Compote, 6", sq. ftd., honey	15.00	Plate, 6½", round.	6.00
Bowl, 8", round nappy	17.50	Compote, 8", ball stem,		Plate, 6½, rnd. finger bowl liner	6.50
Bowl, 9", bell nappy	22.50	sweetmeat	35.00	Plate, 8", rnd.	7.50
Bowl, 9", celery	15.00	Creamer, hexagonal, ftd.	8.50	Plate, 8", rnd., 3 ftd.	12.50
Bowl, 9½", round crimped	25.00	Creamer, low, flat	7.50	Plate, 8½", plain edge	8.00
Bowl, 10", flared	27.50	Creamer, sq. ftd.	8.50	Plate, 8½", rnd.	8.00
Bowl, 10", oval crimped	32.50	Cup	6.00	Plate, 8¾", sq.	8.00

	Amber/Crystal
Plate, 10½", grill, rnd	12.50
Plate, 10", rnd.	12.50
Plate, 10", sq.	12.50
Plate, 12", sq.	20.00
Plate, 15", sq.	30.00
Plate, 14", rnd., torte	27.50
Plate, 20½", rnd., torte	50.00
Plate, cream soup liner, rnd.	5.00
Puff box, w/ cover, 6", rnd.	17.50
Punch bowl	175.00
Punch bowl stand	45.00
Punch cup	6.00
Punch set (bowl, stand, 12 cups, ladle)	300.00
Relish, 8", 3 part	15.00
Saucer, demitasse, rnd.	10.00
Saucer, demitasse, sq.	10.00
Saucer, rnd.	2.00
Saucer, sq.	2.00
Shaker, pr., rnd. ftd.	20.00
Shaker, pr., sq. ftd.	20.00
Stem, 1 oz., rnd. ftd., cordial	12.50
Stem, 1 oz., rnd., ball, cordial	15.00
Stem, 1 oz., sq. ftd., cordial	12.50
Stem, 2 oz., rnd. ftd., wine	10.00
Stem, 2 oz., sq. ftd., wine	10.00
Stem, 2¼ oz., rnd. ball, wine	9.00
Stem, 3 oz., rnd. cocktail	8.00
Stem, 3 oz., sq. ftd., cocktail	8.00
Stem, 3½ oz., rnd. ball, cocktail	7.00

	Amber/Crystal
Stem, 5 oz., rnd. claret	12.50
Stem, 5 oz., sq. ftd., oyster cocktail	9.00
Stem, 8 oz., rnd. water goblet	10.00
Stem, 8 oz., sq. ftd., water goblet	10.00
Stem, sherbet, low, one ball, rnd ftd.	6.00
Stem, sherbet, rnd. low foot	7.00
Stem, sherbet, sq. ftd., low	7.00
Stem. champagne, two ball, rnd ftd.	8.00
Stem. sherbet, high, two ball, rnd ftd.	9.00
Stem. sherbet, rnd. high foot	9.00
Stem. sherbet, sq. ftd., high	9.00
Sugar, hexagonal, ftd.	8.50
Sugar, low, flat	7.50
Sugar, sq. ftd.	8.50
Tid-bit, 2 tier	22.50
Tumbler, 1½ oz., whiskey	10.00
Tumbler, 3 oz., whiskey	9.00
Tumbler, 5 oz., ginger ale	8.00
Tumbler, 5 oz., old fashioned cocktail	10.00
Tumbler, 5 oz., rnd. ftd., ginger ale	8.00
Tumbler, 5 oz., sq. ftd., ginger ale	8.00
Tumbler, 7 oz., rnd. ftd. juice	9.00

	Amber/Crystal
Tumbler, 7 oz., sq. ftd., juice	9.00
Tumbler, 8 oz., rnd., ball, water	10.00
Tumbler, 8 oz., water	10.00
Tumbler, 9 oz., rnd., ball, water	10.00
Tumbler, 9 oz., rnd., ftd. water	10.00
Tumbler, 9 oz., sq. ftd., water	10.00
Tumbler, 10 oz., ice tea	12.00
Tumbler, 11 oz., rnd., ball, ice tea	10.00
Tumbler, 11 oz., sq. ftd., ice tea	12.00
Tumbler, 12 oz., ice tea	12.50
Tumbler, 12½ oz., rnd. ftd. iced tea	10.00
Urn, 11", w/cover	30.00
Vase, 6½", ivy bowl, sq., ftd., crimp top	25.00
Vase, 6½", sq., ftd., flower holder	20.00
Vase, 7½", flip	25.00
Vase, 7½", flip jar w/cover	45.00
Vase, 8", sq. ftd.	35.00
Vase, 8½", flared top	35.00
Vase, 10" (straw jar)	55.00

Please refer to Foreword for pricing information

WESTMORELAND GLASS COMPANY
GRAPEVILLE, PENNSYLVANIA

Handmade Glassware of Quality

Since 1889

WESTMORELAND'S "English Hobnail" Crystal Pattern is handmade in one hundred and thirty-seven open stock items. It is fashioned in three Line Numbers: Line 555 with round foot; Line No. 555/2 has square plates and all stemware items are made with square foot. Line No. 555/3 stemware is barrel-shape, with ball stem and round foot. All three versions are identical in pattern, except for difference in foot as illustrated on the following pages. The various items of all three Lines intermix charmingly, and provide a wide choice for complete luncheon or dinner service.

555/12½ oz. Ice Tea, ftd.
555/9 oz. Tumbler, ftd.
555/7 oz. Tumbler, ftd.
555 Parfait
555 Sherbet High foot.
555 Sherbet Low foot.
555/3 oz. Cocktail
555/8 oz. Goblet

555/5 oz. Claret
555/2 oz. Wine
555 Cordial
555 Old Fashioned Cocktail
1½ oz. Whiskey. Also 3 oz.
555/5 oz. Ginger Ale
555/8 oz. Tumbler
555/10 oz. Ice Tea
555/12 oz. Ice Tea

555/2 oz. Oil
555/6 oz. Oil
555/6 oz. Oil-Vinegar Comb.
555/20 oz. Decanter
555/1 qt. Jug Also in ½ Gal.
555/38 oz. Jug. Also 23 oz., 60 oz.

555 Sugar & Cream Set, footed.
555 Sugar & Cream Set, Low.
555 Salt and Pepper
555/5½ Bell Compote

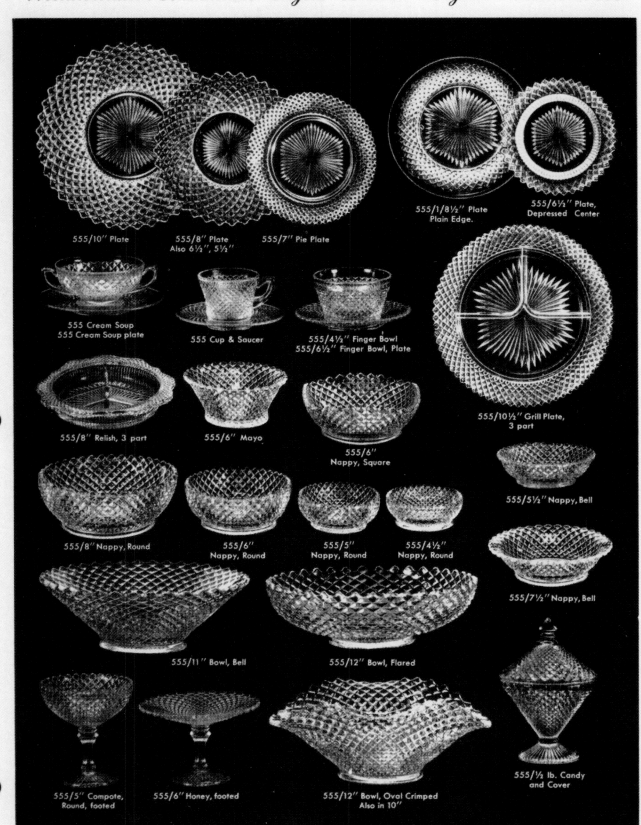

555/10" Plate

555/8" Plate
Also 6½", 5½"

555/7" Pie Plate

555/1/8½" Plate
Plain Edge.

555/6½" Plate,
Depressed Center

555 Cream Soup
555 Cream Soup plate

555 Cup & Saucer

555/4½" Finger Bowl
555/6½" Finger Bowl, Plate

555/10½" Grill Plate,
3 part

555/8" Relish, 3 part

555/6" Mayo

555/6"
Nappy, Square

555/5½" Nappy, Bell

555/8" Nappy, Round

555/6"
Nappy, Round

555/5"
Nappy, Round

555/4½"
Nappy, Round

555/7½" Nappy, Bell

555/11" Bowl, Bell

555/12" Bowl, Flared

555/½ lb. Candy
and Cover

555/5" Compote,
Round, footed

555/6" Honey, footed

555/12" Bowl, Oval Crimped
Also in 10"

555/4½x2½" Cigarette Box & Cover

High Hat

Low Hat

555/4½" Ash Tray.

555 Ind. Nut, ftd.

3" Ash Tray

555 3" Coaster

555/6½" Grapefruit

555/6½" Bon Bon, H'ld.

555/8" Pickle

555/6" Crimped Dish

555/6" Rose Bowl

4" Rose Bowl

555/8"/6 Pt. Bowl. Also in 7"

555/2-Lite Candelabra

555/6" Basket, Tall Handled.

555/6" Three-Footed Covered Dish

555 Marmalade and Cover

555/3½" Candlestick

555/9½" Bowl, Round, Crimped

555/12" Celery, Also 9"

555/14" Torte Plate, Also in 20½"

555/15 Piece Punch Set

555/2/11 oz. Ice Tea, ftd.

555/2/9 oz. Tumbler, ftd.

555/2/7 oz. Tumbler, ftd.

555/2/5 oz. Ginger Ale

555/2/8 oz. Goblet

555/2/3 oz. Cocktail

555/2 Sherbet, Low

555/2 Sherbet, High

555/2/2 oz. Wine

555/2 Cordial

555/2 Oyster Cocktail

555/2 Mustard

555/2 Salt and Pepper

555/2 Cream and Sugar, footed

555/2/5" Compote, Round

555/2/5½" Compote, Bell

555/2/6" Honey, ftd.

555/2/5½" Candlestick

555/2/4½" Nappy, Sq.

555/2 Finger Bowl, footed

555/2 Cup and Saucer

555 Finger Bowl 555/2/6" Sq. Plate

555/2/6" Cheese and Cover. Also 8¾"

555/2/10" Square Plate

555/2/4½" Ash Tray, Sq.

555/2/8¾" Square Plate

555/2/6" Square Plate

555/2/6½" Flower Holder, footed

555/2/6½" Ivy Ball, Crimp Top, ftd.

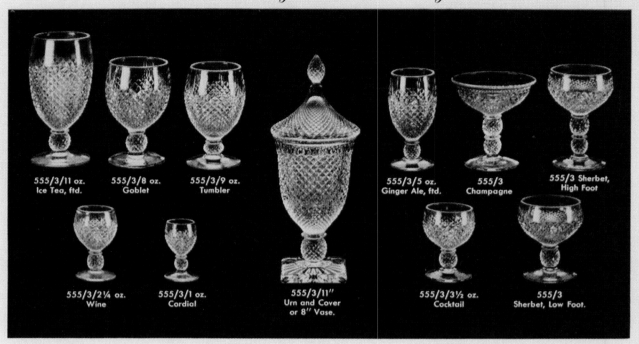

555/3/11 oz. Ice Tea, ftd. 555/3/8 oz. Goblet 555/3/9 oz. Tumbler 555/3/5 oz. Ginger Ale, ftd. 555/3 Champagne 555/3 Sherbet, High Foot

555/3/2¼ oz. Wine 555/3/1 oz. Cordial 555/3/11" Urn and Cover or 8" Vase. 555/3/3½ oz. Cocktail 555/3 Sherbet, Low Foot.

Westmoreland's Handmade "English Hobnail" Crystal

WESTMORELAND has been making their "English Hobnail" Crystal reproductions for more than fifty years. Each piece is made by hand by the same meticulous methods and with the same precise attention to detail that were employed two generations ago.

The scintillating beauty of Westmoreland's old "English Hobnail" Crystal Pattern has long been cherished in many homes. Its charm is a part of gracious living, and the inherent loveliness of its distinctive design increases with long association and use.

"English Hobnail" is adaptable to any decor. It is equally at home in a provincial or modern setting. The wide choice of plates and stemware items make selection a delight. Because it is an open stock pattern you can add to your original selection as you may wish.

WESTMORELAND GLASS COMPANY

GRAPEVILLE, PENNSYLVANIA

Handmade Glassware of Quality

Since 1889

FIRE-KING DINNERWARE "ALICE"
ANCHOR HOCKING GLASS CORPORATION, early 1940's

Colors: Jade-ite, white w/trims of blue or red.

Dinner plates are still the pieces to own in this little "Alice" pattern. I believe that few people bought the plates to go with the cup and saucers that were packed in oatmeal boxes. That was the reason that Hocking's Forest Green Sandwich has six easily found small pieces with all the larger pieces difficult to find. They, too, were packed in "Crystal Wedding Oats." The larger pieces were not premiums, so the marketing procedure failed in these cases at stimulating equal sales of the rest of the pattern.

You will find "Alice" with white plates and with white trimmed in red or blue. Some of the red trimmed pieces fade to pink; and there are two shades of blue trimmed pieces being found. Next time I will show you the red trimmed pieces as I have now found some of that colored trim. I have seen more of the blue or red trimmed "Alice" in Texas than any place else. Of course, it appears to sell best there also!

	Jade-ite	White/Blue trim	White/Red trim
Cup	3.50	8.50	12.50
Plate, 9½"	15.00	17.50	20.00
Saucer	2.00	3.00	5.00

Please refer to Foreword for pricing information

FIRE-KING DINNERWARE CHARM
ANCHOR HOCKING GLASS CORPORATION, 1950-1954

Colors: Azur-ite, Jade-ite, Forest Green and Royal Ruby.

Charm refers to the square shaped dishes made by Anchor Hocking from 1950 through 1954. The Jade-ite and Azur-ite were advertised alongside the Forest Green and Royal Ruby; however, the color names of Forest Green and Royal Ruby prevailed on those squared shapes instead of Charm. Prices for those colors will be found under their respective color names instead of under the pattern name Charm.

I have added some additional pieces including the soup and 9¼" dinner plate. That plate had been listed at 10", but it is not! Although there are fewer collectors of the Jade-ite than the Azur-ite, the scarcity of the Jade-ite has pushed prices for that color above those of the Azur-ite.

The 8⅜" plate is listed in 1950 as a dinner plate, but later as a luncheon plate. Evidently, catalogue writers at Hocking felt that 8⅜" was a very small dinner plate and changed its designation after the first year.

For such a heavily promoted pattern, presently there is a shortage of creamers, sugars, soups, dinner plates and platters in both colors.

	Azur-ite	Jad-ite
Bowl, 4¾", dessert	4.50	7.00
Bowl, 6", soup	12.00	15.00
Bowl, 7⅜", salad	8.00	12.50
Creamer	6.00	10.00
Cup	3.50	7.00
Plate, 6⅝", salad	4.00	4.50
Plate, 8⅜", luncheon	5.00	8.00
Plate, 9¼", dinner	12.00	20.00
Platter, 11" x 8"	12.00	20.00
Saucer, 5⅜"	1.50	2.00
Sugar	6.50	10.00

Please refer to Foreword for pricing information

FIRE-KING DINNERWARE FLEURETTE and HONEYSUCKLE
ANCHOR HOCKING GLASS CORPORATION, 1958-1960

Color: White w/decal.

Fleurette first appears in Anchor Hocking's 1959-1960 catalogue printed in April 1958 and Honeysuckle the following year. Both patterns seem to have given way to Primrose by the 1960-1961 catalogue.

I omitted the snack tray and cup in the last listings even though they are shown in the catalogue listing on page 61. Most of these snack sets were developed for use on the TV fold-up trays so prevalent from the mid 1950's through the 1960's.

Since leaching of lead in better crystal and china is coming under increased scrutiny, I might caution you that lead based paint was used on patterns during this time also. So if you consider using them daily, proceed with caution! They say acidic wines can leach lead from costly lead crystal in as little as twenty minutes. So be cautious in putting acidic foods on top of painted designs for long periods of time. Remember the big clamor over some fast food chain's giveaway cartoon glasses in the early 1980's. These dishes used the same type process in their manufacture.

I have enclosed catalogue sheets for Fleurette on pages 60-62 and Honeysuckle on page 63. Note on page 61 the various sized sets of Fleurette that were available: 16 pc., 19 pc., 35 pc., and 53 pc. On page 62, you can see the actual selling prices of these sets when they were first issued.

There were three sizes of tumblers listed for the Honeysuckle set, but none were listed for Fleurette. In all my travels the last two years, I have seen very little Honeysuckle offered for sale — at any price! You might bear that in mind if you see some priced reasonably.

	Fleurette	Honeysuckle
Bowl, 4⅝", dessert	2.00	2.00
Bowl, 6⅝", soup plate	3.50	4.00
Bowl, 8¼", vegetable	8.00	8.00
Creamer	43.00	4.00
Cup, 5 oz., snack	2.00	
Cup, 8 oz.	3.50	4.00
Plate, 6¼", bread and butter	1.50	
Plate, 7⅜", salad	2.50	3.00
Plate, 9⅛", dinner	3.50	4.50
Platter, 9" x 12"	10.00	10.00
Saucer, 5¾"	.50	.50
Sugar	3.00	3.00
Sugar cover	3.00	3.00
Tumbler, 5 oz., juice		3.50
Tumbler, 9 oz., water		4.50
Tumbler, 12 oz., iced tea		6.00
Tray, 11"x 6", snack	2.50	

FLEURETTE® DINNERWARE

W4679/58 — W4629/58

W4674/58

W4637/58 — W4638/58 — W4641/58

PACKING

W4679/58—8 oz. Cup	6 doz. — 25 lbs.
W4629/58—5 ¾ " Saucer	6 doz. — 27 lbs.
W4674/58—4 ⅝ " Dessert	6 doz. — 21 lbs.
W4637/58—6 ¼ " Bread & Butter Plate	3 doz. — 16 lbs.
W4638/58—7 ⅜ " Salad Plate	3 doz. — 23 lbs.
W4641/58—9 ⅛ " Dinner Plate	3 doz. — 39 lbs.

W4667/58

Fleurette
Prepacked Sets
are shown on
Page 3.

W4647/58

W4667/58— 6 ⅝ " Soup Plate	3 doz. — 27 lbs.
W4647/58—12 x 9" Platter	1 doz. — 20 lbs.

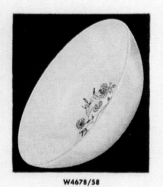

W4678/58

See Prepacked
Serva-Snack Set
on Page 3.

W4653/58 — W4654/58

W4678/58—8 ¼ " Vegetable Bowl	1 doz. — 15 lbs.
W4653/58— Sugar & Cover	2 doz. — 16 lbs.
W4654/58— Creamer	2 doz. — 12 lbs.

HEAT-PROOF

FLEURETTE® PREPACKED SETS

W4600/4—16 Pce. Starter Set
Each Set in Gift Display Carton,
4 Sets to Shipping Carton — 37 lbs.
COMPOSITION:
Four W4679/58 Cups
Four W4629/58 Saucers
Four W4674/58 Desserts
Four W4641/58 Dinner Plates

W4600/2—35 Pce. Dinner Set
Each Set in Shipping Carton — 21 lbs.
COMPOSITION:
Six W4679/58 Cups   One W4678/58 Vegetable Bowl
Six W4629/58 Saucers   One W4647/58 Platter
Six W4674/58 Desserts   One W4653/58 Sugar & Cover
Six W4638/58 Salad Plates   One W4654/58 Creamer
Six W4641/58 Dinner Plates

W4600/1—19 Pce. Luncheon Set (Not Illustrated)
Each Set in Gift Carton, 4 Sets to Shipping Carton — 41 lbs.
COMPOSITION:
Four W4679/58 Cups   Four W4641/58 Dinner Plates
Four W4629/58 Saucers   One W4653/58 Sugar & Cover
Four W4674/58 Desserts   One W4654/58 Creamer

W4600/3—53 Pce. Dinner Set (Not Illustrated)
Each Set in Shipping Carton — 32 lbs.
COMPOSITION:
Eight W4679/58 Cups   Eight W4641/58 Dinner Plates
Eight W4629/58 Saucers   One W4678/58 Vegetable Bowl
Eight W4674/58 Desserts   One W4647/58 Platter
Eight W4638/58 Salad Plates   One W4653/58 Sugar & Cover
Eight W4667/58 Soup Plates   One W4654/58 Creamer

SERVA-SNACK SET

W4600/9—8 Pce. Snack Set
Each Set in Die-Cut Display Carton,
6 Sets to Shipping Carton — 48 lbs.
COMPOSITION:
Four 5 oz. Cups
Four 11 x 6" Rectangular Trays

(See Crystal Serva-Snack Sets on Page 10.)

PROMOTE PREPACKED SETS

HEAT-PROOF

Fleurette

W4647/58

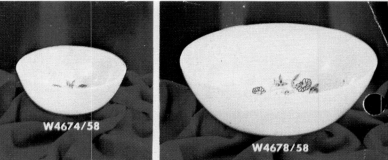

W4674/58

W4678/58

HEAT-PROOF

W4667/58

W4653/58

W4679/58 — W4629/58

W4654/58

Anchorglass ®

OPEN STOCK		Per Doz. Net Pkd.	Doz. Ctn.	Wt. Ctn.
W4679/58—	8 oz. Cup	$ .90	6	25#
W4629/58—	5¾" Saucer	.90	6	28#
W4674/58—	4⅝" Dessert	.90	6	21#
W4637/58—	6¼" B & B Plate	1.20	3	16#
W4638/58—	7⅜" Salad Plate	1.50	3	23#
W4667/58—	6⅝" Soup Plate	1.60	3	24#
W4641/58—	9⅛" Dinner Plate	1.80	3	39#
W4678/58—	8¼" Vegetable Bowl	2.40	1	14#
W4647/58—	12 x 9" Platter	3.60	1	20#
W4653/58—	Sugar & Cover	1.50	2	11#
W4654/58—	Creamer	1.25	2	12#

SETS

W4600/4—16 PCE. STARTER SET $1.55 Set 4 Sets 39#
(Each Set in Gift Display Ctn.)
COMPOSITION: Four each Cups, Saucers, Desserts and Dinner Plates

W4600/1—19 PCE. LUNCHEON SET 1.75 Set 4 Sets 40#
(Each Set in Gift Carton)
COMPOSITION: Four each Cups, Saucers, Desserts and Dinner Plates. One Sugar & Cover and one Creamer.

W4600/2—35 PCE. DINNER SET 3.95 Set 1 Set 21#
(Each Set in Shipping Carton)
COMPOSITION: Six each Cups, Saucers, Desserts, Salad Plates and Dinner Plates. One each Vegetable Bowl, Platter, Sugar & Cover and Creamer.

W4600/3—53 PCE. DINNER SET 6.00 Set 1 Set 32#
(Each Set in Shipping Carton)
COMPOSITION: Eight each Cups, Saucers, Desserts, Salad Plates, Soup Plates and Dinner Plates. One each Vegetable Bowl, Platter, Sugar & Cover and Creamer.

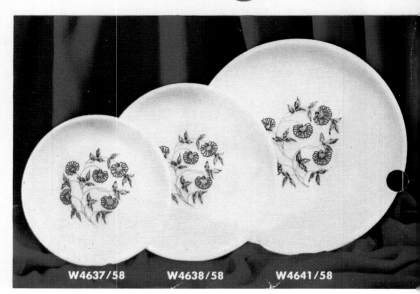

W4637/58   W4638/58   W4641/58

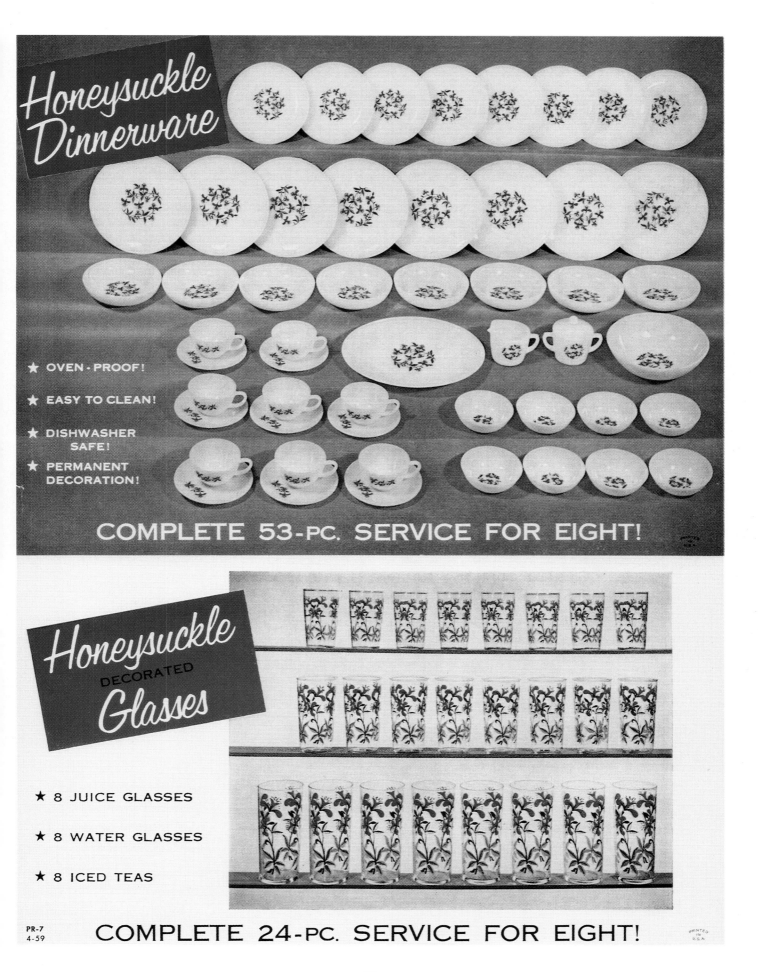

Honeysuckle Dinnerware

★ OVEN-PROOF!

★ EASY TO CLEAN!

★ DISHWASHER SAFE!

★ PERMANENT DECORATION!

COMPLETE 53-PC. SERVICE FOR EIGHT!

Honeysuckle DECORATED Glasses

★ 8 JUICE GLASSES

★ 8 WATER GLASSES

★ 8 ICED TEAS

COMPLETE 24-PC. SERVICE FOR EIGHT!

PR-7
4-59

FIRE-KING DINNERWARE "GAME BIRD"
ANCHOR HOCKING GLASS CORPORATION, 1959-1962

Color: White w/decal decoration.

Anchor Hocking called these both "Wild Bird" and "Game Bird," but the "Game Bird" seemed more apropos when I was making a decision which to use for the first *Collectible Glassware from the 40's, 50's, 60's ....* Since that time, other authors have used the name; so I guess my choice "inspired" their work.

I have catalogue sheets of mugs, cereals and ash trays listed for 1960-1961, but as you can see below, there are many more pieces available than those.

You will find the following birds on this pattern: "Canada Goose," "Ringed-Necked Pheasant," "Ruffled Grouse" and "Mallard Duck."

I have chosen to show only the Ringed Neck Pheasant in my photograph this time. Actually, I have come to believe that this is the only "game" in town on serving pieces. If you have any other "Game Bird" on the sugar, creamer, 8¼" vegetable or platter, let me know. It is possible to collect a whole set of Pheasant decorated dinnerware, but no other bird can be collected in a full set as far as I can determine. (That is my educated guess until one of you readers can send me information otherwise.)

Prices on this little pattern have taken a dramatic rise due to the number of collectors searching for these feathered friends. There is quite an interest in collecting this more macho set among the males who used to be dragged to Depression glass shows, so they could pay for the purchases and tote them to the car. Now, there are many of these former "toters" who are also spenders. If there were enough birds flushed to make everyone happy, then we could all have pheasant under glass! Unfortunately, there aren't enough of these feathered friends to suit everyone looking for them!

	White w/decals
Ash tray, 5¼"	5.50
Bowl, 4⅝", dessert	4.00
Bowl, 5", soup or cereal	6.50
Bowl, 8¼", vegetable	15.00
Creamer	7.00
Mug, 8 oz.	8.00
Plate, 7⅜", salad	4.00
Plate, 9⅛", dinner	6.50
Platter, 12" x 9"	15.00
Sugar	6.00
Sugar cover	3.00
Tumbler, 11 oz., iced tea	7.50

Please refer to Foreword for pricing information

64

Anchorwhite heat-resistant Mugs and Bowls

ANCHORGLASS

With authentic game bird decorations

Colorful game bird decorations lend a touch of rustic charm to these practical Anchorwhite mugs and bowls. The mugs are as ideal for in-home use as they are for outdoors. Versatile, too, they're perfect for coffee as well as for cocoa, hot chocolate and milk. The cereal-soup bowls, with their matching decorations, will brighten up any table setting. Both mugs and bowls are heat-resistant and safe to use with hot liquids and foods.

No.	Size	Item	Doz. Ctn.	Lbs. Ctn.
W1212/5931	8 oz.	Ruffed Grouse Mug	4	27
W1212/5932	8 oz.	Ring-Necked Pheasant Mug	4	27
W1212/5933	8 oz.	Canada Goose Mug	4	27
W1212/5934	8 oz.	Mallard Duck Mug	4	27
W291/5931	5"	Ruffed Grouse Bowl	4	27
W291/5932	5"	Ring-Necked Pheasant Bowl	4	27
W291/5933	5"	Canada Goose Bowl	4	27
W291/5934	5"	Mallard Duck Bowl	4	27

ANCHOR HOCKING GLASS CORPORATION
Lancaster, Ohio, U.S.A.

FIRE-KING DINNERWARE JADE-ITE RESTAURANT WARE
ANCHOR HOCKING GLASS CORPORATION, 1950-1956

Jade-ite collectors are adding to their other Hocking sets with the Restaurant Ware line. Several pieces are in increasingly short supply due to avid gatherings of this line. The smaller platter (9½") is rapidly disappearing. The 5-compartment plate and the oval partitioned plates (already discontinued before 1953) are not being seen as regularly as many collectors would wish. Thankfully, not every collector wants these pieces.

This Restaurant Ware line of Anchor Hocking is being sought also for its adaptability to microwave use. As far as I know, any of these pieces can be used this way. Remember to put the dish in the microwave for just a little time to see if it gets hot as you would test any other dish. "Jane Ray" collectors started the rush on this Jade-ite and now there is not enough of this short-lived pattern to go around.

You can see a catalogue sheet on page 68 to show you the differences in the three sizes of cups and the mug. This mug seems to come in both thick and thin styles.

	Jade-ite		Jade-ite
Bowl, 4¾", fruit G294	5.00	Plate, 8⅞", oval partitioned G211	8.50
Bowl, 8 oz., flanged rim, cereal G305	10.00	Plate, 8", luncheon G316	5.00
Bowl, 10 oz., deep G309	8.00	Plate, 9⅝", 3-compartment G292	6.00
Bowl, 15 oz., deep G300	10.00	Plate, 9⅝", 5-compartment G311	15.00
Cup, 6 oz., straight G215	5.00	Plate, 9¾", oval, sandwich G216	10.00
Cup, 7 oz., extra heavy G299	6.00	Plate, 9", dinner G306	8.00
Cup, 7 oz., narrow rim G319	6.00	Platter, 9½", oval G307	12.50
Mug, coffee, 7 oz. G212	7.00	Platter, 11½", oval G308	10.00
Plate, 5½", bread/butter G315	2.00	Saucer, 6" G295	2.00
Plate, 6¾", pie or salad G297	4.00		

Please refer to Foreword for pricing information

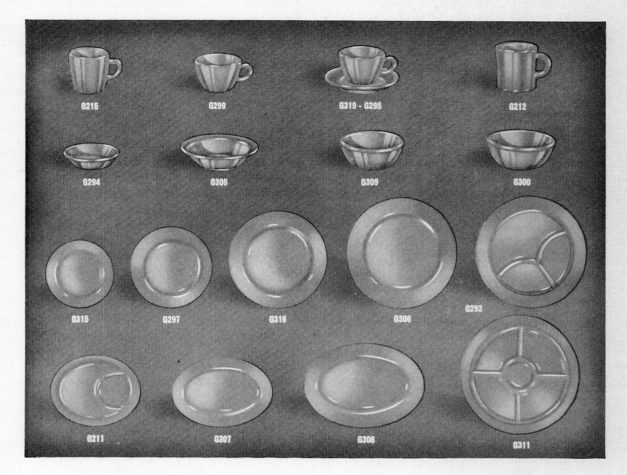

A COMPLETE SERVICE FOR MASS FEEDING ESTABLISHMENTS

Cat. No.	Description	Actual Size or Capacity	Std. Pkg.	Weight
G215	Cup (Straight)	6 oz.	4 doz.	35#
G299	Cup (Extra Heavy)	7 oz.	4 doz.	36#
G319	Cup (Narrow Rim)	7 oz.	4 doz.	32#
G295	Saucer	6"	4 doz.	31#
G212	Coffee Mug (Extra Heavy)	7 oz.	4 doz.	48#
G294	Fruit	4¾"	6 doz.	30#
G305	Grapefruit—Cereal	8 oz.	4 doz.	37#
G309	Bowl	10 oz.	4 doz.	30#
G300	Bowl	15 oz.	4 doz.	43#
G315	B & B Plate	5½"	4 doz.	30#
G297	Pie or Salad Plate	6¾"	4 doz.	35#
G316	Luncheon Plate	8"	2 doz.	26#
G306	Dinner Plate	9"	2 doz.	31#
G292	3-Compartment Plate	9⅝"	2 doz.	38#
G211	Oval Partitioned Plate	8⅞"	2 doz.	23#
G307	Oval Platter	9½"	2 doz.	24#
G308	Oval Platter	11½"	1 doz.	20#
G311	5-Compartment Plate	9⅝"	2 doz.	37#

*REG. U. S. PAT. OFF.

PRINTED IN U.S.A.

ANCHOR HOCKING GLASS CORP.
LANCASTER, OHIO, U. S. A.

FIRE-KING DINNERWARE "JANE RAY"
ANCHOR HOCKING GLASS CORPORATION, 1945-1963

Colors: Ivory, Jade-ite, Peach Lustre, white and white trimmed in gold.

"Jane Ray" has always been considered to be made in Jade-ite only. In fact, I had it listed in only Jade-ite in my first book. Notice that there **ARE** other colors that can be found. I have only found the demitasse cup and saucers in Peach Lustre and white, but there may be other pieces available. Be on the lookout!

"Jane Ray" is a name that collectors have called this pattern. A 1947 chain store listing of glassware by Anchor Hocking lists this as "Jade-ite Heat Proof Tableware," which is the only real name known. This listing also records the vegetable bowl as 8⅛" instead of 8¼" as listed in later catalogues.

"Jane Ray" is one of the most collected Anchor Hocking patterns from this era. A Jade-ite set is still possible to attain in this dinnerware, and many collectors are using the Restaurant Ware line to supplement "Jane Ray." Demitasse sets are the most difficult pieces to find with collectors grudgingly giving up nearly thirty dollars for them. Remember that the saucers are harder to find than the cups. These may be the Iris demitasse sets of tomorrow! Platters and soup bowls are also becoming scarce for this normally easy to find pattern.

Availability, as with blue Bubble and green Block years ago, puts this pattern in front of many new collectors. Prices are rising, however, due to the ever increasing demand and the difficulty of locating some pieces. If you like this pattern, start collecting now and spring for the harder to find pieces when you find them! You won't be sorry!

	Ivory/White	Jade-ite
Bowl, 4⅞", dessert	3.50	4.50
Bowl, 5⅞", oatmeal	7.50	7.00
Bowl, 7⅝", soup plate	10.00	13.00
Bowl, 8¼", vegetable	12.00	12.00
Cup	4.00	3.00
Cup, demitasse	13.50	13.50
Creamer	7.50	4.50
Plate, 7¾", salad	7.00	6.00
Plate, 9⅛", dinner	9.00	7.50
Platter, 9" x 12"	12.00	11.00
Saucer	1.50	1.50
Saucer, demitasse	15.00	15.00
Sugar	5.00	4.00
Sugar cover	2.50	6.00

FIRE-KING DINNERWARE PEACH LUSTRE/GRAY LAUREL
ANCHOR HOCKING GLASS CORPORATION, 1952-1963

"The New Sensation" is how Peach Lustre color/pattern was described in a 1952 catalogue. This "laurel leaf" design was also made as Gray Laurel in 1953. A 1953 catalogue is the only time that Gray Laurel is mentioned in Hocking records. I suspect that gray will turn out to be rather scarce when compared to the quantity of Peach Lustre ("laurel leaf" design) that continued until the 1963 catalogue. Page 70 is taken from a 1954 catalogue. From its introduction until its demise in 1963, the name Peach Luster was used for the **color** and not just the pattern. The 11" serving plate was discontinued as of 8-25-60.

I have seen very little Gray Laurel since the set I found in Phoenix several years ago. Gray Laurel has three sizes of tumblers that were made to go with it. These tumblers are "complementary decorated" with gray and maroon bands. There is a 5 ounce juice, a 9 ounce water and a 13 ounce iced tea. To date, I have not spotted any of these.

Catalogue numbers are the same for each pattern with Gray Laurel having a "K" prefix and Peach Lustre using an "L" prefix.

The crystal stemware shown under Bubble and "Boopie" was also engraved with a "Laurel" cutting to go with these patterns. Only crystal pieces have this cutting of one band of leaves.

	Gray Laurel	Peach Lustre		Gray Laurel	Peach Lustre
Bowl, 4⅞", dessert	4.00	3.00	Plate, 7⅜", salad	4.00	3.00
Bowl, 7⅝", soup plate	5.00	5.00	Plate, 9⅛", dinner	7.50	4.00
Bowl, 8¼", vegetable	8.50	7.50	Plate, 11", serving	12.00	9.00
Creamer, ftd.	4.50	3.50	Saucer, 5¾"	.75	.75
Cup, 8 oz.	4.00	3.50	Sugar, ftd.	4.50	3.50

Peach Lustre Dinnerware

HEAT-RESISTANT

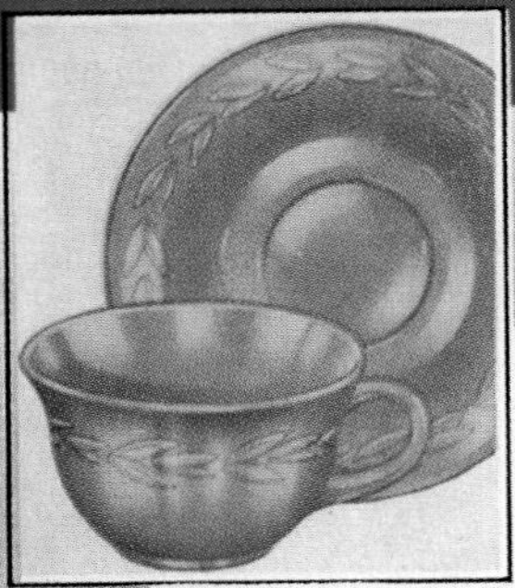

L4379 — L4329

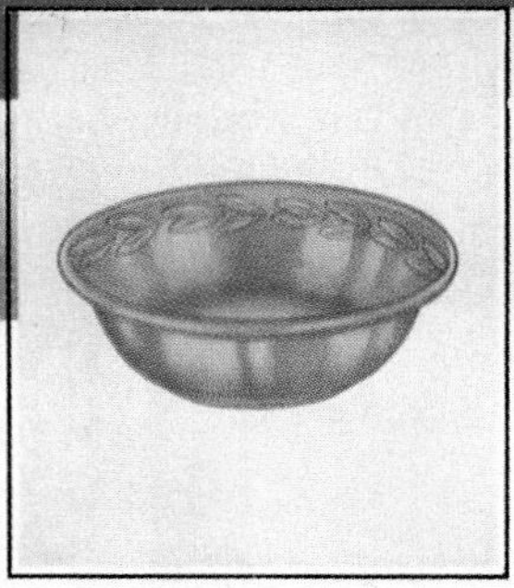

L4374

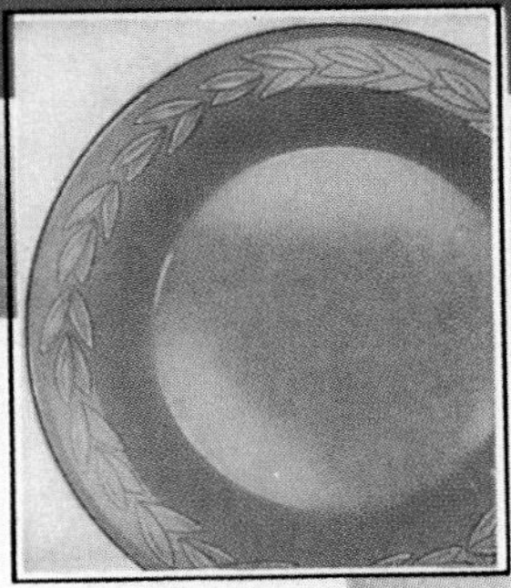

L4338 — L4341

		PACKING
L4379—8 oz.	Cup	6 doz. — 25 lbs.
L4329—5 3/4"	Saucer	6 doz. — 27 lbs.
L4374—4 7/8"	Dessert	6 doz. — 25 lbs.
L4338—7 3/4"	Salad Plate	3 doz. — 28 lbs.
L4341—9 1/8"	Dinner Plate	3 doz. — 37 lbs.

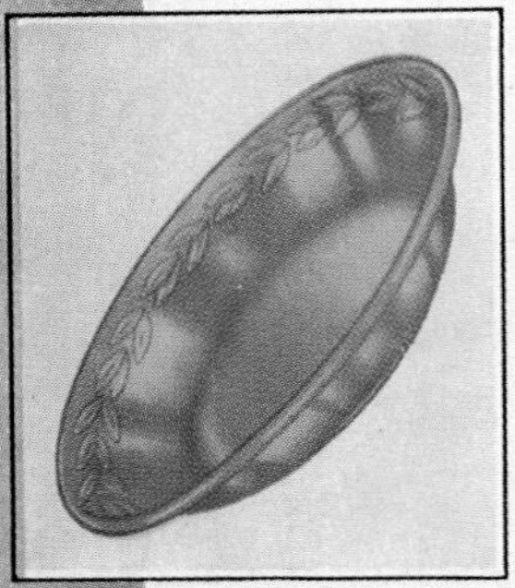

L4367

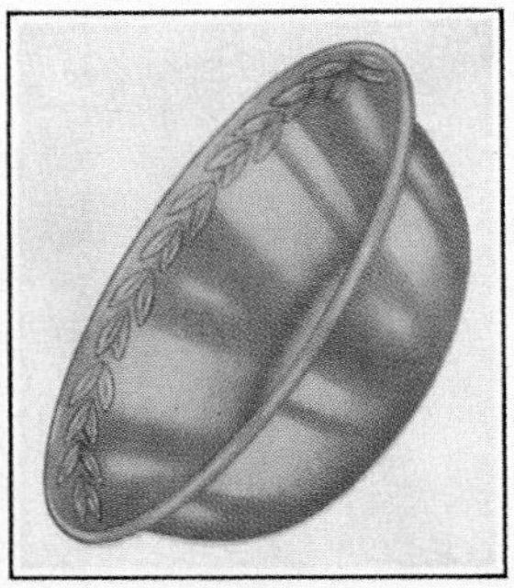

L4378

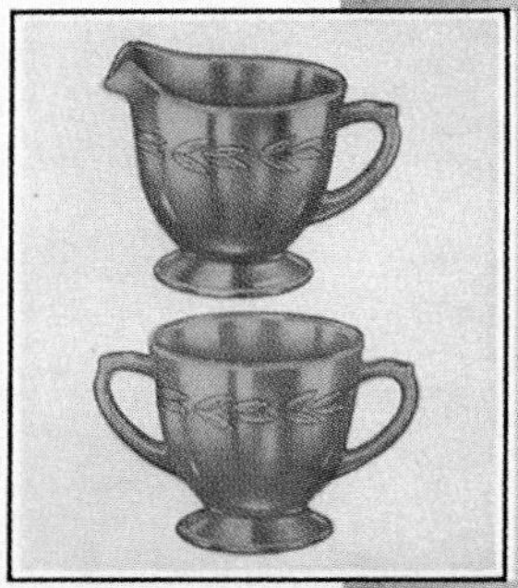

L4353 — L4354

L4367—7 5/8"	Soup Plate	3 doz. — 29 lbs.
L4378—8 1/4"	Vegetable Bowl	1 doz. — 14 lbs.
L4353—	Sugar	2 doz. — 11 lbs.
L4354—	Creamer	2 doz. — 10 lbs.

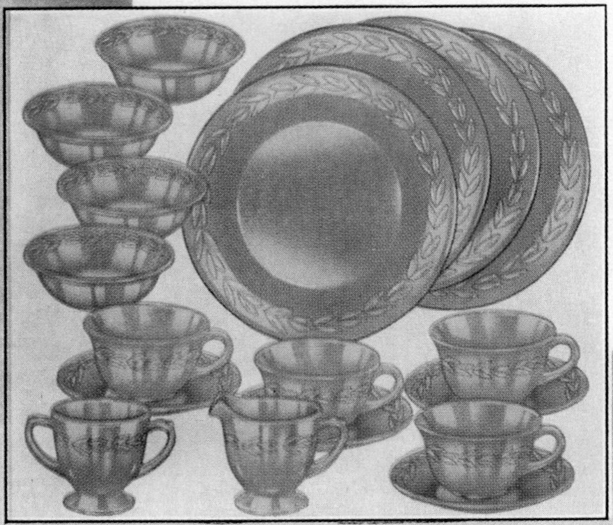

L4300/33

PREPACKED SET

L4300/33—18 Pce. Luncheon Set

Each Set in Gift Carton, 4 Sets to Shipping Carton — 41 lbs.

COMPOSITION:

Four L4379 Cups
Four L4329 Saucers
Four L4374 Desserts
Four L4341 Dinner Plates
One L4353 Sugar
One L4354 Creamer

PROMOTE SETS

FIRE-KING DINNERWARE & OVENWARE PRIMROSE
ANCHOR HOCKING GLASS CORPORATION, 1960-1962

Primrose was the pattern that Anchor Hocking used to bridge the gap between dinnerware and ovenware usage. Primrose was made for both with pieces designed for both jobs. Although many of Anchor Hocking's lines were issued as dinnerware, they are marked ovenware on the bottom to let customers know that they were "heat-proof" and could be "pre-warmed" in the oven.

Primrose seems to be the pattern that Hocking marketed more than they did Fleurette and Honeysuckle; but Primrose may not have been as successful as many earlier Fire-King patterns. It was only listed in the 1960-1961 and 1961-1962 catalogues. From the availability I see in the ovenware line, it might be scarce or, as with the blue Fire-King ovenware, many housewives are still using it!

All casserole covers are clear crystal Fire-King. All pieces of ovenware were guaranteed against oven breakage for two years. Dealers would exchange a new item for the broken pieces. The one quart casserole, baking pan and oval casserole were all sold with a brass finished candle warmer and candle. I have received numerous letters saying that these brass holders are still working as they were intended!

The deep loaf pan was sold as a baking pan by adding a crystal glass cover.

	White w/decal			White w/decal			White w/decal	
Bowl, 4⅝", dessert	2.00		Casserole, 2 qt., knob cover	12.50		Plate, 7⅜", salad	2.50
Bowl, 6⅝", soup plate	5.00		Creamer	4.00		Plate, 9⅛", dinner	5.00
Bowl, 8¼", vegetable	7.00		Cup, 5 oz., snack	2.50		Platter, 9" x 12"	12.00
Cake pan, 8", round	8.50		Cup, 8 oz.	3.00		Saucer, 5¾"	1.00
Cake pan, 8", square	8.50		Custard, 6 oz., low or dessert	3.00		Sugar	3.50
Casserole, pt., knob cover	6.50		Pan, 5" x 9", baking, w/cover	12.50		Sugar cover	2.50
Casserole, ½ qt., oval, au gratin cover	14.00		Pan, 5" x 9", deep loaf	10.00		Tray, 11" x 6", rectangular, snack	4.00
Casserole, 1 qt., knob cover	10.00		Pan, 6½" x 10½", utility baking	9.00		Tumbler, 5 oz., juice	4.00
Casserole, 1½ qt., knob cover	10.00		Pan, 8" x 12½", utility baking	12.50		Tumbler, 9 oz., water	5.00
			Plate, 6¼", bread and butter	1.50		Tumbler, 13 oz., iced tea	6.00

Please refer to Foreword for pricing information

NEW!
Primrose
Anchorwhite heat-resistant ovenware

The delicate red, tan and grey tones of stylized flowers enhance this new gleaming white ovenware. It's glamorous . . . on the table . . . in the kitchen. It's perfect for special occasions or everyday use . . . just right for oven-to-table service, storing and reheating. Build more colorful displays with this eye-catching, traffic-stopping, Primrose Ovenware. It will sell on sight! Available in 8 and 11 piece sets in gift cartons . . . also in open stock.

ANCHOR HOCKING GLASS CORPORATION
Lancaster, Ohio, U. S. A.

W407/62

W467/62

W408/62

W469/62

W406/62

W405/62

W424/62

W410/62

W411/62

W409/62

W452/62

W450/62

New
Primrose
Anchorglass
Ovenware

Number	Size	Item	Doz. Ctn.	Lbs. Ctn.
W424/62	6 Oz.	Dessert	4	15
W405/62	1 Pt.	Casserole, Cover	1	16
W406/62	1 Qt.	Casserole, Cover	½	14
W407/62	1½ Qt.	Casserole, Cover	½	19
W467/62	1½ Qt.	Oval Casserole, Au Gratin Cover	½	19
W408/62	2 Qt.	Casserole, Cover	½	21
W450/62	8"	Round Cake Pan	½	12
W452/62	8"	Square Cake Pan	½	17
W409/62	5" x 9"	Deep Loaf Pan	½	11
W410/62	6½" x 10½"	Utility Baking Pan	½	15
W411/62	8" x 12½"	Utility Baking Pan	½	23
W469/62	5" x 9"	Baking Pan and Cover	½	21
W400/245*		8 Pc. Set	4 Sets	34
W400/246**		11 Pc. Set	4 Sets	53

*Composition: One each 1 qt. Casserole, Cover, 10½" Utility Baking Pan, 8" Round Cake Pan; four 6 oz. Desserts, Gift Ctn.

**Composition: One each 1½ qt. Casserole, Cover, 5" x 9" Deep Loaf Pan, 8" x 12½" Utility Baking Pan, 8" Square Cake Pan; six 6 oz. Desserts, Gift Ctn.

FIRE-KING OVEN GLASS ANCHOR HOCKING GLASS CORPORATION, 1942-1950's

Colors: Sapphire blue, crystal; some Ivory and Jade-ite.

Fire-King is still one of the more easily recognized patterns in this book! Every household has a piece or two. Many have more! It was the ovenware that was recognized for its endurance. Fire-King had a two year guarantee to back up the durability of all its oven proof glassware. All you had to do was take the broken pieces to your local dealer and that piece was replaced at no charge.

Fire-King is fine for normal ovens, but it tends to develop heat cracks from sudden temperature changes when used in the microwave. Cathy used to make her oatmeal that way, and the bowls would crack as they cooled off.

The dry cup measure has ounce measurements up the side and no spout for pouring. Without **these measurements on the side**, it is the normally found mug!

The reason that juice saver pie plates are so high in price comes from the fact that most were heavily used. Many are deeply scratched. To obtain the price below, this pie plate has to be mint!

The skillet and nipple cover on page 75 are shown compliments of Anchor-Hocking's photographer. The skillets are still in hiding, but a few nipple covers have surfaced. These blue covers are embossed "BINKY'S NIP CAP U.S.A." (and not Fire-King). The boxed set on page 76 has a Fire-King measuring cup, nipple cover, measuring spoons and nipples. The side of the box reads "Binky Formula Feeding Set, Glass Measuring Cup, Glass Nipple Protector, Plastic Funnel, Plastic Scoop, 4 Plastic Measuring Spoons, Binky Baby Products Co., NY., U.S.A." The brochure enclosed in the box states "BINKYTOYS — The Best for Baby for over a Quarter Century. BINKYTOYS meet every advocated requirement essential to baby's SAFETY - HEALTH — and WELL BEING."

The prices with asterisks under Ivory are for Jade-ite items with the Fire-King **embossing**. All the Ivory is plain with no design. You will find plain Ivory and Jade-ite mugs, but they hold eight oz. and not seven. The Jade-ite mug with the embossed Fire-King pattern is rare!

All listings below are from Anchor Hocking's Catalogue "L" with some additional catalogue items shown on page 77.

There are two styles of table servers being found; and you can find a casserole lid on top of a Bersted Mfg. Co. popcorn popper. One of these can be seen in the fourth edition of my *Kitchen Glassware of the Depression Era*.

	Ivory	Sapphire		Ivory	Sapphire
Baker, 1 pt., 4½" x 5"		5.50	Loaf pan, 9⅛" x 5⅛", deep	13.50	20.00
Baker, 1 pt., round	4.00	5.00	Mug, coffee, 7 oz., 2 styles	*27.50	23.00
Baker, 1 qt., round	6.00	7.00	Nipple cover		150.00
Baker, 1½ qt., round	6.00	12.00	Nurser, 4 oz.		15.00
Baker, 2 qt., round	8.50	12.50	Nurser, 8 oz.		23.00
Baker, 6 oz., individual	3.00	5.00	Percolator top, 2⅛"		5.00
Bowl, 4⅜", individual pie plate		12.00	Pie plate, 8⅜", 1½" deep		7.50
Bowl, 5⅜", cereal or deep dish pie plate	6.50	13.00	Pie plate, 9⅝", 1½" deep		9.50
Bowl, measuring, 16 oz.		23.00	Pie plate, 9", 1½" deep	7.00	8.50
Cake pan (deep), 8¾" (½ roaster)		22.50	Pie plate, 10⅜", juice saver	*70.00	70.00
Cake pan, 9"	13.00		Refrigerator jar & cover, 4½" x 5"	**8.00	11.00
Casserole, 1 pt., knob handle cover	8.50	12.00	Refrigerator jar & cover, 5⅛" x 9⅛"	**16.00	32.50
Casserole, 1 qt., knob handle cover	10.00	12.50	Roaster, 8¾"		45.00
Casserole, 1 qt., pie plate cover		16.00	Roaster, 10⅜"		67.50
Casserole, 1½ qt., knob handle cover	12.00	13.00	Table server, tab handles (hot plate)	9.00	16.00
Casserole, 1½ qt., pie plate cover		17.00	Utility bowl, 6⅞", 1 qt.		12.00
Casserole, 2 qt., knob handle cover	13.50	20.00	Utility bowl, 8⅜", 1½ qt.		16.00
Casserole, 2 qt., pie plate cover		25.00	Utility bowl, 10⅛"		18.00
Casserole, individual, 10 oz.		13.00	Utility pan, 8⅛" x 12½", 2 qt.		35.00
Cup, 8 oz. measuring, 1 spout		17.00	Utility pan, 10½" x 2" deep	12.50	22.50
Cup, 8 oz., dry measure, no spout		155.00			
Cup, 8 oz., measuring, 3 spout		20.00	***Jade-ite w/embossed design**		
Custard cup or baker, 5 oz.	3.00	3.25	****Jade-ite**		
Custard cup or baker, 6 oz.	3.25	4.00			

Please refer to Foreword for pricing information

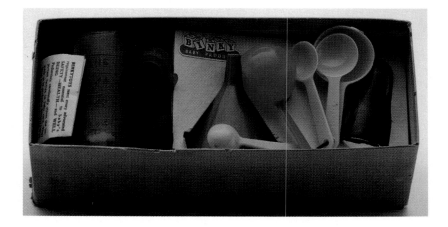

FIRE - KING OVEN GLASS

Housewives prefer to cook in glass for they are then able to actually see their foods cooking, eliminating the possibility of improperly cooked foods. Glass is also more easily cleaned than metal utensils, saving time and labor.

A three-fold purpose—bake, serve, and store in the same dish. Fire-King oven glass is not only suitable for oven cooking but makes ideal serving dishes for the table and in addition is safe and practical for refrigerator use.

Not only does Fire-King possess unusual cooking qualities but it is attractive, a complement to any table, and above all—the lowest priced oven glass on the market.

77

FIRE-KING OVEN WARE, TURQUOISE BLUE
ANCHOR HOCKING GLASS CORPORATION, 1957-1958

Color: Turquoise Blue.

Turquoise Blue was advertised as dinnerware, but all pieces are marked ovenware. Most of Anchor Hocking's dinnerware is also marked ovenware. This let the customer know that the glassware could be pre-warmed in the oven before serving. Turquoise Blue has become as popular a pattern as the Fire-King Sapphire blue oven glass. When you search for and use a pattern for five years as we did this one, several observations about buying or using it come to mind. The 10" plates are rare and not available in quantity. As far as I am concerned, it is an ideal size for a dinner plate. (The normal 9" dinner did not hold enough for my boys with its upturned edges.) Soup and cereal bowls are not commonly found and are probably under priced in today's market.

On a personal note, we retired the Turquoise blue several years ago and started using another more modern blue pattern. Nothing had been said about the change until before Christmas when Marc, my college sophomore asked why we had quit using his "favorite dishes." (We had kept a chipped 8" vegetable bowl to use and it was dirty. This 8" bowl was always the one my kids used as their soup or cereal bowl. Now he had no clean soup bowl and it was time for an explanation!) When he opened a box for Christmas, there were three of these bowls for his own start on Turquoise Blue. We had no idea they were his "favorite dishes!"

The batter bowl was never shown in catalogues. I recently received a call from a lady who had been told that Hocking only made eight of these and she had better buy the one offered her for more than $150.00. What a sales pitch! No one knows how many of any one piece of glass was made — not even the glass factories themselves!

The 5¾" ash tray was discontinued before the 1957-58 catalogue was out of print. There were special promotions of the three part relish, egg plate and the snack sets with 22K gold decorations. Do not put these gold edged pieces in the microwave because the gold causes sparks. All other pieces worked well in our microwave.

Cups, saucers, 9" dinner plates, creamer and sugar are easily found. Mugs are the next easiest pieces to accumulate. The 6⅛" and 7" plates are not quite as hard to find as the 10" plates, but they are both uncommon. Numerous collectors have told me they have never seen either one! Although the 9" plates with cup indent is not as plentiful as the dinner plate, it does not command the price of the dinner since not every buyer wants to own snack sets... yet! The 1 qt. round mixing bowl and the 3 qt. tear shaped mixing bowls are the most difficult sizes to find in these four-bowl sets. The 1 qt. tear shaped bowl is always the first to sell at shows. Many people want these as small serving dishes.

	Blue		Blue
Ash tray, 3½"	6.50	Bowl, round, mixing, 3 qt.	12.00
Ash tray, 4⅝"	9.00	Bowl, round, mixing, 4 qt.	14.00
Ash tray, 5¾"	13.00	Creamer	6.00
Batter bowl, w/spout	65.00	Cup	4.00
Bowl, 4½", berry	6.00	Egg plate, 9¾"	15.00
Bowl, 5", cereal	12.00	Mug, 8 oz.	10.00
Bowl, 6⅝", soup/salad	15.00	Plate, 6⅛"	10.00
Bowl, 8", vegetable	14.00	Plate, 7"	11.00
Bowl, tear, mixing, 1 pt.	11.00	Plate, 9"	7.00
Bowl, tear, mixing, 1 qt.	15.00	Plate, 9", w/cup indent	7.00
Bowl, tear, mixing, 2 qt.	18.00	Plate, 10"	26.00
Bowl, tear, mixing, 3 qt.	20.00	Relish, 3 part, 11⅛"	12.00
Bowl, round, mixing, 1 qt.	11.00	Saucer	1.00
Bowl, round, mixing, 2 qt.	9.00	Sugar	6.00

Please refer to Foreword for pricing information

TURQUOISE-BLUE TABLEWARE — HEAT-PROOF

B4079 — B4029

B4074

B4037 — B4038 — B4041 — B4046

		PACKING	
B4079—	8 oz. Cup	6 doz. —	24 lbs.
B4029—	5 ¾ " Saucer	6 doz. —	32 lbs.
B4074—	4 ⅝ " Dessert	6 doz. —	23 lbs.
B4037—	6 ¼ " Bread & Butter Plate	3 doz. —	18 lbs.
B4038—	7 ¼ " Salad Plate	3 doz. —	23 lbs.
B4041—	9 " Dinner Plate	3 doz. —	42 lbs.
B4046—	10 " Serving Plate	1 doz. —	18 lbs.

See Mixing Bowls on Page 27, Mug and Bowl on Page 23 and Ash Trays on Page 41.

B4067

B4078

B4053 — B4054

B4067—	6 ⅝ " Soup Plate	3 doz. —	26 lbs.
B4078—	8 ¼ " Vegetable Bowl	1 doz. —	17 lbs.
B4053—	Sugar	2 doz. —	11 lbs.
B4054—	Creamer	2 doz. —	11 lbs.

B4000/18

PREPACKED SETS

B4000/18—12 Pce. Starter Set
Each Set in Display Style Carton, 6 Sets to Shipper — 48 lbs.
COMPOSITION: Four Each B4079 Cups, B4029 Saucers and B4041 Dinner Plates

B4000/19—18 Pce. Luncheon Set
Each Set in Gift Carton, 4 Sets to Shipper — 40 lbs.
COMPOSITION: Four Each B4079 Cups, B4029 Saucers, B4074 Desserts, and B4041 Dinner Plates; One Each B4053 Sugar and B4054 Creamer

B4000/21—34 Pce. Dinner Set
Each Set in Shipping Carton — 20 lbs.
COMPOSITION: Six Each B4079 Cups, B4029 Saucers, B4074 Desserts, B4038 Salad Plates and B4041 Dinner Plates; One Each B4078 Vegetable Bowl, B4046 Serving Plate, B4053 Sugar and B4054 Creamer

B4000/22—52 Pce. Dinner Set
Each Set in Shipping Carton — 32 lbs.
COMPOSITION: Eight Each B4079 Cups, B4029 Saucers, B4074 Desserts, B4038 Salad Plates, B4067 Soup Plates and B4041 Dinner Plates; One Each B4078 Vegetable Bowl, B4046 Serving Plate, B4053 Sugar and B4054 Creamer

FIRE-KING OVEN WARE, "SWIRL" ANCHOR HOCKING GLASS CORPORATION, 1950's

Colors: Azur-ite, Ivory, Ivory trimmed in gold or red, white or white trimmed in gold, and Pink.

To repeat from the first book: "I looked at the many "swirled" patterns that Anchor Hocking made starting with 1950 and spent a whole day trying to find a way to organize them into some sequence of order that made a little sense. First of all, **colors** determined name and not pattern which has been a major problem with Anchor Hocking. There were also two distinct swirled patterns and even a change in sugar styles. Finally, I came up with the following for this book: Swirls of the 1950's and Swirls of the 1960's."

The first "Swirl" introduced in 1950 was Azur-ite which is the light blue shown on top of page 83; that was followed by Sunrise (red trimmed, shown on bottom of page 83). In 1953, Ivory White was introduced; but in the mid 1950's, this became known as Anchorwhite. If you find a flat white sugar or creamer, it is Ivory White; but finding a footed creamer or sugar means it is Anchorwhite. Golden Anniversary was introduced in 1955 by adding 22K gold trim to Ivory White; and Pink was not introduced until 1956.

Note the footed sugar and creamer in pink. These do not have the typical white exteriors normally found on the bottoms of this pattern. Tumblers were made to go with only the pink as far as I can find out.

	Anchorwhite Ivory White	Golden Anniversary	Azur-ite/Pink Sunrise
Bowl, 4⅞", fruit or dessert	2.50	2.75	4.00
Bowl, 7¼", vegetable			10.00
Bowl, 7⅝", soup plate	2.75	3.00	7.00
Bowl, 8¼", vegetable	5.00	5.00	12.00
Creamer, flat	3.50		7.00
Creamer, ftd.	2.75	3.25	
Cup, 8 oz.	2.75	3.00	5.00
Plate, 7⅜", salad	2.50	2.50	4.00
Plate, 9⅛", dinner	3.00	4.00	6.50
Plate, 11", serving			15.00
Platter, 12" x 9"	6.00	6.50	13.00
Saucer, 5¾"	.50	.50	1.50
Sugar lid, for flat sugar	2.50		5.00
Sugar lid, for ftd. sugar	2.50		
Sugar, flat, tab handles	3.50		6.00
Sugar, ftd., open handles	3.00	3.50	
Tumbler, 5 oz., juice			4.50
Tumbler, 9 oz., water			6.00
Tumbler, 12 oz., iced tea			6.50

Please refer to Foreword for pricing information

GOLDEN ANNIVERSARY DINNERWARE

W4100/57—18 Pce. Luncheon Set
Each Set in Gift Carton, 4 Sets to Shipping Carton — 41 lbs.
COMPOSITION:

Four W4179/50 Cups	Four W4141/50 Dinner Plates
Four W4129/50 Saucers	One W4153/50 Sugar
Four W4174/50 Desserts	One W4154/50 Creamer

W4100/58—34 Pce. Dinner Set (Not illustrated)
Each Set in Shipping Carton — 23 lbs.
COMPOSITION:

Six W4179/50 Cups	One W4178/50 Vegetable Bowl
Six W4129/50 Saucers	One W4147/50 Platter
Six W4174/50 Desserts	One W4153/50 Sugar
Six W4138/50 Salad Plates	One W4154/50 Creamer
Six W4141/50 Dinner Plates	

W4100/59—52 Pce. Dinner Set (Not illustrated)
Each Set in Shipping Carton — 35 lbs.
COMPOSITION:

Eight W4179/50 Cups	Eight W4141/50 Dinner Plates
Eight W4129/50 Saucers	One W4178/50 Vegetable Bowl
Eight W4174/50 Desserts	One W4147/50 Platter
Eight W4138/50 Salad Plates	One W4153/50 Sugar
Eight W4167/50 Soup Plates	One W4154/50 Creamer

W4100/57

OPEN STOCK

W4179/50 — W4129/50   W4174/50   W4138/50 — W4141/50   W4167/50

			PACKING
W4179/50—		Cup	6 doz. — 26 lbs.
W4129/50—		Saucer	6 doz. — 28 lbs.
W4174/50—4 ⅞"	Dessert		6 doz. — 24 lbs.
W4138/50—7 ¾"	Salad Plate		3 doz. — 26 lbs.
W4141/50—9 ⅛"	Dinner Plate		3 doz. — 40 lbs.
W4167/50—7 ⅝"	Soup Plate		3 doz. — 29 lbs.

W4178/50   W4147/50   W4153/50 — W4154/50

W4178/50— 8 ¼"	Vegetable Bowl		1 doz. — 15 lbs.
W4147/50—12 x 9"	Platter		1 doz. — 21 lbs.
W4153/50—	Sugar		2 doz. — 10 lbs.
W4154/50—	Creamer		2 doz. — 10 lbs.

HEAT-PROOF   **ANCHORWHITE — 22 K. GOLD TRIMMED**

PINK Anchorglass® DINNERWARE

M4179 — M4129

M4174

M4138 — M4141 — M4146

M4167

			PACKING	
M4179—	8 oz.	Cup	6 doz. —	25 lbs.
M4129—	5 ¾″	Saucer	6 doz. —	32 lbs.
M4174—	4 ⅞″	Dessert	6 doz. —	25 lbs.
M4138—	7 ¾″	Salad Plate	3 doz. —	27 lbs.
M4141—	9 ⅛″	Dinner Plate	3 doz. —	38 lbs.
M4146—	11″	Serving Plate	1 doz. —	20 lbs.
M4167—	7 ⅝″	Soup Plate	3 doz. —	29 lbs.

DESIGNED FOR BEAUTY — PRICED FOR EVERYDAY VOLUME SALES.

M4177 — M4178

M4143 — M4144

M4177—	7 ¼″	Vegetable Bowl	1 doz. —	11 lbs.
M4178—	8 ¼″	Vegetable Bowl	1 doz. —	15 lbs.
M4143—		Sugar & Cover	2 doz. —	11 lbs.
M4144—		Creamer	2 doz. —	12 lbs.

Each Piece comes with a beautiful Pink, Black and Gold
label reading "PINK HEAT-PROOF ANCHORGLASS."

See Listing of Prepacked Sets on Page 2.

— HEAT-PROOF —

FIRE-KING OVEN WARE, "SWIRL"
ANCHOR HOCKING GLASS CORPORATION, 1960's-1975

Colors: White, white trimmed in gold, Jade-ite, and iridized Lustre.

Anchorwhite "Swirl" continued to be made into the early 1960's. In 1963, Hocking changed the "Swirl" by making the edge more scalloped. This new design with the 22K. gold edge was called Golden Shell when introduced; and it was made into the late 1970's. Pages 86 and 87 show catalogue pages of this new design. Note the taller footed creamer and sugar in this line.

You can see the major differences in Golden Anniversary on page 82 and Golden Shell on page 87 by studying these catalogue reprints. These two patterns do not blend as well as some similar patterns since the serving pieces are decidedly more scalloped on the Golden Shell's serving pieces. The cups, creamers and sugars are also shaped so they do not blend as well.

Using this new "Swirl" design, Anchor Hocking introduced a Jade-ite set in 1964. The catalogue called it an "English Regency style." You can see an example of this pattern on the bottom of page 88. To continue the confusion, this had no real name except Jade-ite. It was listed in catalogues until 1972.

In 1966, Lustre Shell was introduced and manufactured until the late 1970's. This iridized color was the same used for Peach Lustre, first introduced in 1952. Since Peach Lustre was discontinued in 1963, someone at Hocking must have missed spraying on that color. Of course, marketing gurus may have decided the public needed an iridized color again.

The soup bowl was sized upward from 6⅜" to 7⅝" with the reintroduction of this color. Lustre was Anchor Hocking's name for the color and shell was the design. Now why didn't they add shell to the Jade-ite and solve our name problems thirty years later? "Jade-ite Shell" has a nice ring, don't you think?

A demitasse cup and saucer were introduced to the Lustre Shell line in 1972. As with other Fire-King patterns, the demitasse saucers are harder to find than the cups.

On page 89 are two photographs of "Swirl" with hand painted scenes. I thought the glass was priced right for what it was and the few pieces of hand painted Pyrex in with the Anchor Hocking Ware didn't deter me from buying it in the least little way. This set was purchased from an antique mall in Zanesville, Ohio. I was told by the shop owner that the artist was a lady who had worked at the Fenton factory. Diagnosed with cancer, she returned home to paint dishes as her hobby. Some pieces are hand signed J. Kinney. I have contacted Frank Fenton at the Fenton factory and there are no records of a J. Kinney having ever decorated glassware for Fenton. If anyone else should know J. Kinney or has any information about this, please contact me. I received a number of letters from collectors trying to talk me out of this set!

	Golden Shell	Jade-ite "Shell"	Lustre Shell
Bowl, 4¾", dessert	1.75	3.00	3.00
Bowl, 6⅜", cereal	2.50	4.00	4.50
Bowl, 7⅝", soup plate	5.00	6.00	5.00
Bowl, 6⅜", soup	4.00	4.50	
Bowl, 8½", vegetable	5.50	6.00	8.00
Creamer, ftd.	3.50	5.50	5.50
Cup, 8 oz.	3.25	4.00	4.00
Cup, 3¼ oz., demitasse			7.00
Saucer, 4¾", demitasse			5.50
Plate, 7¼", salad	2.50	2.75	3.50
Plate, 10", dinner	4.00	6.00	7.00
Platter, 9½" x 13"	8.00	12.00	
Saucer, 5¾"	.50	.50	.50
Sugar, ftd.	2.75	6.00	6.00
Sugar cover	4.00	4.00	4.00

W2379/31 — W2329/31   W2374/31   W2338/31 — W2346/31

PACKING

				PACKING
W2379/31—		Cup		3 doz. — 14 lbs.
W2329/31—	5¾"	Saucer		3 doz. — 13 lbs.
W2374/31—	4¾"	Dessert		3 doz. — 13 lbs.
W2338/31—	7¼"	Salad Plate		3 doz. — 23 lbs.
W2346/31—	10"	Dinner Plate		3 doz. — 43 lbs.

HEAT

RESISTANT

W2367/31   W2378/31

W2367/31—	6⅜"	Soup Plate		3 doz. — 22 lbs.
W2378/31—	8½"	Vegetable Bowl		1 doz. — 15 lbs.

HEAT-RESISTANT — ANCHORWHITE — 22 K. GOLD TRIMMED

W2347/31   W2353/31 — W2354/31

W2347/31—	13 x 9½"	Platter		1 doz. — 22 lbs.
W2353/31—		Sugar & Cover		1 doz. — 9 lbs.
W2354/31—		Creamer		1 doz. — 6 lbs.

HEAT-RESISTANT

Golden Shell Dinnerware Sets

16-PIECE
STARTER
SET
GIFT-BOXED

ANCHORWHITE
EDGED
WITH 22 K.
GOLD

W2300/1—16 Pce. Starter Set

Each Set in Gift Display Box, 4 Sets to Shipping Carton — 38 lbs.

COMPOSITION:
Four W2379/31 Cups
Four W2329/31 Saucers
Four W2374/31 Desserts
Four W2346/31 Dinner Plates

HEAT-RESISTANT

35-PIECE
SET
WITH 22 K. GOLD

53-PIECE
SET LISTED
BELOW

W2300/2

W2300/2—35 Pce. Dinner Set

Each Set in Shipping Carton — 23 lbs.

COMPOSITION:
Six W2379/31 Cups
Six W2329/31 Saucers
Six W2374/31 Desserts
Six W2367/31 Soups
Six W2346/31 Dinner Plates
One W2378/31 Vegetable Bowl
One W2347/31 Platter
One W2353/31 Sugar & Cover
One W2354/31 Creamer

W2300/3—53 Pce. Dinner Set

Each Set in Shipping Carton — 33 lbs.

COMPOSITION:
Eight W2379/31 Cups
Eight W2329/31 Saucers
Eight W2374/31 Desserts
Eight W2338/31 Salad Plates
Eight W2367/31 Soups
Eight W2346/31 Dinner Plates
One W2378/31 Vegetable Bowl
One W2347/31 Platter
One W2353/31 Sugar & Cover
One W2354/31 Creamer

FIRE-KING OVEN WARE, WHEAT & BLUE MOSAIC
ANCHOR HOCKING GLASS CORPORATION, 1962-late 1960's

Blue Mosaic's photograph was slightly anemic last time with only a platter to show. I have been able to find pieces of Blue Mosaic in Florida as I travel. This short lived Anchor Hocking pattern was shown only in a 1967 catalogue. There is a snack tray with cup added to the listing. The same blue cup accompanies the snack tray as is shown on a saucer in the photograph. No designed cups were made as far as I can determine.

Wheat production began in 1962 and was one of Anchor Hocking's most productive lines of the 1960's. Like Sapphire blue Fire-King in the 1940's, everyone has seen the Wheat pattern of the 1960's!

Both the oval and round 1½ quart casseroles and the 10½" baking pan were used with candle warmers. These candle warmers were brass finished with walnut handles and candle. A few of these warmers have been seen with prices in the $4.00 to $5.00 range. Most of these were never used as they are being found with the candles intact!

	Wheat	Blue Mosaic		Wheat	Blue Mosaic
Bowl, 4⅝", dessert	2.50	3.50	Cup, 8 oz.	3.00	
Bowl, 6⅝", soup plate	4.50	5.50	Custard, 6 oz., low or dessert	2.50	
Bowl, 8¼", vegetable	6.00	10.00	Pan, 5" x 9", baking, w/cover	12.50	
Cake pan, 8", round	8.00		Pan, 5" x 9", deep loaf	8.00	
Cake pan, 8", square	8.00		Pan, 6½" x 10½" x 1½",		
Casserole, 1 pt., knob cover	5.00		utility baking	9.00	
Casserole, 1 qt., knob cover	7.50		Pan, 8" x 12½" x 2",		
Casserole, 1½ qt., knob cover	9.50		utility baking	11.00	
Casserole, 1½ qt., oval,			Plate, 7⅜", salad	2.50	4.00
au gratin cover	12.50		Plate, 10", dinner	4.00	6.00
Casserole, 2 qt., knob cover	12.50		Platter, 9" x 12"	9.00	15.00
Casserole, 2 qt., round,			Saucer, 5¾"	1.00	1.50
au gratin cover	14.00		Sugar	3.00	5.00
Creamer	4.00	5.00	Sugar cover	3.50	3.50
Cup, 5 oz., snack	3.00		Tray, 11" x 6", rectangular, snack	3.50	3.50
Cup, 7½ oz.		4.50			

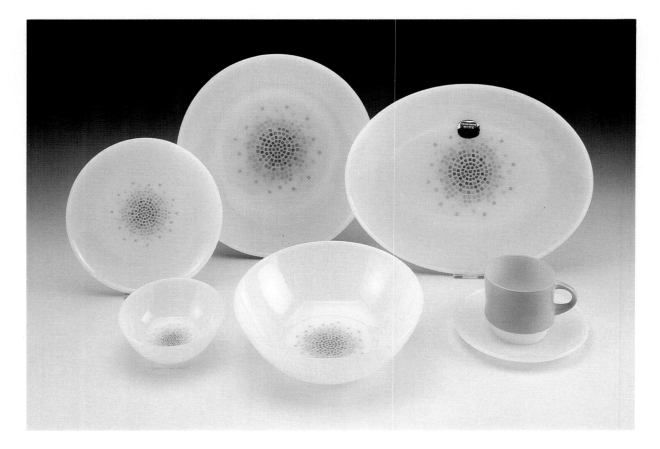

Wheat Anchorwhite Dinnerware

W4679/65 — W4629/65

W4674/65

W4638/65 — W4646/65

		PACKING	
W4679/65— 8 oz. Cup		3 doz. — 14 lbs.	
W4629/65— 5¾" Saucer		3 doz. — 14 lbs.	
W4674/65— 4⅝" Dessert		3 doz. — 11 lbs.	
W4638/65— 7⅜" Salad Plate		3 doz. — 23 lbs.	
W4646/65—10" Dinner Plate		3 doz. — 44 lbs.	

W4667/65

W4678/65

W4667/65—6⅝" Soup Plate		3 doz. — 25 lbs.	
W4678/65—8¼" Vegetable Bowl		1 doz. — 14 lbs.	

HEAT-RESISTANT

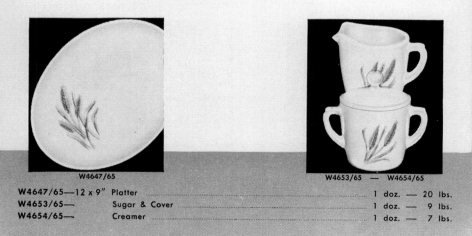

W4647/65

W4653/65 — W4654/65

W4647/65—12 x 9" Platter		1 doz. — 20 lbs.	
W4653/65— Sugar & Cover		1 doz. — 9 lbs.	
W4654/65— Creamer		1 doz. — 7 lbs.	

See Prepacked Sets on Page 13.

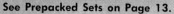

Wheat Anchorwhite Ovenware

W424/65

W405/65 — W406/65

W407/65 — W408/65

PACKING

W424/65—6	oz.	Dessert or Low Custard	4 doz. — 14 lbs.
W405/65—1	Pt.	Casserole—Knob Cover	1 doz. — 16 lbs.
W406/65—1	Qt.	Casserole—Knob Cover	½ doz. — 14 lbs.
W407/65—1 ½	Qt.	Casserole—Knob Cover	½ doz. — 19 lbs.
W408/65—2	Qt.	Casserole—Knob Cover	½ doz. — 22 lbs.

All Covers are Clear Crystal Fire-King.

W467/65

W450/65

W452/65

W467/65—1 ½	Qt.	Casserole—Au Gratin Cover	½ doz. — 18 lbs.
W450/65—8"		Round Cake Pan	½ doz. — 12 lbs.
W452/65—8"		Square Cake Pan	½ doz. — 17 lbs.

GUARANTEED 2 YEARS AGAINST OVEN BREAKAGE.

To be replaced Free by dealer in exchange for broken pieces.

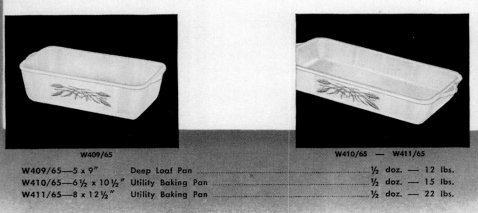

W409/65

W410/65 — W411/65

W409/65—5 x 9"		Deep Loaf Pan	½ doz. — 12 lbs.
W410/65—6 ½ x 10 ½"		Utility Baking Pan	½ doz. — 15 lbs.
W411/65—8 x 12 ½"		Utility Baking Pan	½ doz. — 22 lbs.

"Fire-King" — The World's Finest Baking Ware. Also available in Crystal, Anchorwhite and Copper-Tint.

Wheat Ovenware Sets

W400/313—8 Pce. Ovenware Set

Each Set in Gift Carton, 4 Sets to Shipping Carton — 34 lbs.

COMPOSITION:
One W406/65 Casserole—Knob Cover
One W410/65 Utility Baking Pan
One W450/65 Round Cake Pan
Four W424/65 Desserts or Custards

"Fire-King" — The World's Finest Baking Ware. Also available in Crystal, Anchor-white and Copper-Tint.

W400/314—11 Pce. Ovenware Set

Each Set in Gift Carton, 4 Sets to Shipping Carton — 53 lbs.

COMPOSITION:
One W407/65 Casserole—Knob Cover
One W409/65 Deep Loaf Pan
One W411/65 Utility Baking Pan
One W452/65 Square Cake Pan
Six W424/65 Desserts or Custards

W400/315—Round Casserole & Candlewarmer Set

Each Set in Gift Carton, 4 Sets to Shipping Carton — 20 lbs.

COMPOSITION:
One W407/65 Casserole & Crystal Cover
One Brass Finished Candlewarmer
(Candle included)

W400/317—Oval Casserole & Candlewarmer Set

Each Set in Gift Carton, 4 Sets to Shipping Carton — 19 lbs.

COMPOSITION:
One W467/65 Oval Casserole & Crystal Cover
One Brass Finished Candlewarmer
(Candle included)

W400/316—Baking Pan & Candlewarmer Set

Each Set in Gift Carton, 4 Sets to Shipping Carton — 18 lbs.

COMPOSITION:
One W410/65 Utility Baking Pan
One Brass Finished Twin Candlewarmer
(Candle included)

HEAT-RESISTANT

93

FLORAGOLD, "LOUISA" JEANNETTE GLASS COMPANY, 1950's

Colors: Iridescent, some Shell Pink, ice blue and crystal.

Floragold is one of the patterns that formerly was in *The Collector's Encyclopedia of Depression Glass*. Since this pattern was made long after the Depression era, it now resides comfortably in this book. Most often Floragold is confused with an old Carnival glass pattern called Louisa. Some "antique dealers" who do not sell much glassware will price this early 1950's glassware "out of sight." Carnival glass collectors most often accept glassware made through the 1920's. The rose bowl in Carnival "Louisa" is often offered for sale as Floragold which turns the confusion around the other way.

The prices on Floragold vases have finally steadied. Make sure the one you are buying has good iridized color. For such a large investment, you do not need a weakly sprayed-on color. This vase was made by taking the 15 oz. tumbler and fluting the top. These large, 15 oz. tumblers can be found in crystal selling in the $10.00 range, but add the iridized spray and you are rapidly approaching a "Ben Franklin." Crystal tumblers were sprayed with the iridized color and refired to make it stay. Evidently, many of these tumblers were never sprayed. Occasionally, you will see a crystal vase. That is enough to make you try to learn how to iridize glassware!

There are two different 5¼" comports in Floragold. Both of these are pictured in the first edition of my *Very Rare Glassware of the Depression Years* book. One has a ruffled top, and the other has a plain top. You can see the ruffled comport below as a pattern shot.

Perfect tops to shakers are hard to find. They were made of plastic, and many were broken by tightening them too much. Only white or brown plastic tops are originals. Each top is worth $15.00; so more than half of the price of the shakers is for the tops!

Because cups were sold without saucers in two ways, there are an abundance of cups in Floragold. The large bowl and the pitcher were both sold with twelve cups as "egg nog" sets for the Christmas market. Each set sold added another dozen to the cup production; so, today, saucers have a right to be scarce. That 5¼" saucer has no cup ring and is the same as the sherbet plate.

Ice blue, crystal, red-yellow, Shell Pink and iridized large size comports were made in the late 1950's and into the early 1970's. See Shell Pink for a look at the shape of this piece. All the other colored comports are **selling** in the $10.00 range and **sitting** on the shelf at any price from $15.00 up. I just saw an iridized comport for sale at a flea market for $175.00, and they were willing to take $145.00 "today only!"

	Iridescent
Ash tray/coaster, 4"	5.50
Bowl, 4½", square	5.50
Bowl, 5½", round cereal	32.50
Bowl, 5½", ruffled fruit	8.00
Bowl, 8½", square	13.00
Bowl, 9½", deep salad	37.50
Bowl, 9½", ruffled	8.00
Bowl, 12", ruffled large fruit	7.00
Butter dish and cover, ¼ lb. oblong	24.00
Butter dish and cover, round, 6¼" sq. base	40.00
Butter dish bottom	13.50
Butter dish top	26.50
Butter dish and cover, round, 5½" sq. base	625.00
Candlesticks, double branch, pr.	47.50
Candy dish, 1 handle	11.00
Candy or Cheese dish and cover, 6¾"	47.50
*Candy, 5¼" long, 4 feet	7.50
Comport, 5¼", plain top	575.00
Comport, 5¼", ruffled top	675.00
Creamer	9.00
Cup	6.00
Pitcher, 64 oz.	35.00
Plate or tray, 13½"	20.00
Plate or tray, 13½", with indent	47.50
Plate, 5¼", sherbet	12.00
Plate, 8½", dinner	35.00
Platter, 11¼"	20.00
**Salt and pepper, plastic tops	47.50
Saucer, 5¼" (no ring)	12.00
Sherbet, low, footed	14.00
Sugar	6.50
Sugar lid	10.00

	Iridescent
Tid-bit, wooden post	32.50
Tumbler, 10 oz., footed	18.00
Tumbler, 11 oz., footed	18.00
Tumbler, 15 oz., footed	90.00
Vase or celery	350.00

* Shell pink $20.00
**Tops $15.00 each included in price

Please refer to Foreword for pricing information

FOREST GREEN ANCHOR HOCKING GLASS COMPANY CORPORATION, 1950-1967

Color: Forest Green.

Forest Green is actually the color made by Anchor Hocking and not a pattern. Forest Green started out using the square **Charm** blank in 1950, but the glassware became better known by its color. Even Hocking's "Bubble" was called Forest Green as you can see by the catalogue sheet on page 19.

The bottom of page 16 shows some stemware that was sold along with Bubble. These have been called "Boopie" by collectors, but in the last two years the prices of the Forest Green "Boopie" have steadily declined while the "Bubble stemware" shown on page 19 has increased in price. I think it has more to do with the quantities of "Boopie" being found than any other reason. These lines are both priced below.

An oval vegetable in Forest Green has been found. This bowl is scalloped along the edges and has a swirled effect on the sides. See this bowl on right of picture on page 97. Several large quantities of this bowl and the platter have appeared recently and the price for both of these items has softened somewhat. It is hard to convince customers that these pieces are hard to find when some dealers insist on setting them out in stacks of twenty or more when they buy a large supply. I have seen this four times in the last year. This is bad marketing or showing-off. There is a fine line in any case!

For a pattern made so late, 6" soup bowls and dinner plates are infrequently found. At least one listing of the 8⅜" plate was as a dinner plate, so perhaps that is why 9¼" dinners are so hard to find. That plate had been listed at 10" previously, but it is not! Were the larger plates made as an after thought?

You will find many odd dark green pieces on the market. To be truly Forest Green, it has to have been made by Anchor Hocking!

The large quantity of 4" ball ivy vases testifies to successful sales of Citronella candles that were packed in these vases. The picture shows a boxed set of two "mosquito repellent" candles that originally sold for $1.19. Having been in Florida most of the last few years makes me want to find a few cases of these for my boat dock and porch. Since the screened porch is now my office, I have had a problem with my lights on after dark. Since I put in fourteen to sixteen hour days, I have not found a way to work in daylight only. Besides, I have to fish sometime! Mosquitoes cover the windows on the outside until there is no more room! It takes a vacuum cleaner to dispose of all the bodies. (Blind mosquitoes they may be called, but they gravitate to light!) They hit the screens and sound like rain! It beats shoveling snow on Christmas Day as I did over the holidays when I went back to Kentucky. Vacuuming mosquitoes that do not bite, beats shoveling snow any day!

One reader reported finding a box of twenty-four 7 oz. tumblers in a box marked, "Clover Honey Delight, Packed by National Honey Packers Mt. Sterling Illinois." She never said whether they contained honey or not.

The jumbo iced tea has been corrected to read 15 oz. instead of 19 oz. I left out the quart jumbo iced tea in my prices last time; it is now included. Decorated tumblers such as "A Bicycle for Two" will bring a dollar or two more than regular tumblers when they sell. Undecorated tumblers sell faster to collectors!

	Green		Green		Green
Ash tray, 3½", square	3.70	Stem, 6 oz., sherbet	9.00	Tumbler, 10 oz., ftd., 4½"	6.50
Ash tray, 4⅝", square	5.00	*Stem, 6 oz., sherbet	6.00	Tumbler, 11 oz.	7.00
Ash tray, 5¾", square	7.00	*Stem, 9 oz., goblet	10.00	Tumbler, 13 oz., iced tea	7.50
Ash tray, 5¾", hexagonal	8.00	Stem, 9½ oz., goblet	13.00	Tumbler, 14 oz., 5"	7.50
Batter bowl w/spout	20.00	*Stem, 14 oz., iced tea	14.00	Tumbler, 15 oz., long boy	8.50
Bowl, 4¾", dessert	5.50	Sugar, flat	6.50	Tumbler, 15 oz., tall iced tea	12.00
Bowl, 5¼" deep	8.50	Tumbler, 5 oz., 3½"	4.00	Tumbler, 32 oz, giant iced tea	15.00
Bowl, 6", soup	16.00	Tumbler, 7 oz.	4.00	Vase, 4" ivy ball	3.50
Bowl, 6", mixing	9.00	Tumbler, 9 oz., table	5.00	Vase, 6⅜"	4.50
Bowl, 7⅜", salad	11.00	Tumbler, 9 oz., fancy	6.00	Vase, 9"	6.50
Bowl, 8½", oval vegetable	20.00	Tumbler, 9½ oz., tall	6.50		
Creamer, flat	6.50			* "Boopie"	
Cup (square)	5.00				
Pitcher, 22 oz.	22.50				
Pitcher, 36 oz.	25.00				
Pitcher, 86 oz., round	27.50				
Plate, 6¾", salad	5.00				
Plate, 6⅝", salad	5.00				
Plate, 8⅜", luncheon	6.00				
Plate, 9¼", dinner	27.50				
Platter, 11", rectangular	22.00				
Punch bowl	22.50				
Punch bowl stand	22.50				
Punch cup (round)	2.25				
Saucer, 5⅜"	1.50				
Sherbet, flat	7.00				
*Stem, 3½ oz., cocktail	10.00				
*Stem, 4 oz., juice	10.00				
Stem, 4½ oz., cocktail	12.50				
Stem, 5½ oz., juice	12.50				

Please refer to Foreword for pricing information

GOLDEN GLORY FEDERAL GLASS COMPANY, 1959-66; 1978-79

Color: White with 22K gold decorations.

Golden Glory, a small Federal pattern, is beginning to show up in collecting circles. The 22K gold decorations wear easily as detergent will fade them. This makes for difficulty in finding mint condition pieces. Dishes were bought to be used, and using them caused wear marks that collectors today have to take into account.

Originally, there were a dozen pieces issued. When reissued in 1978, there were three pieces added. This later issue included the larger 10" dinner plate, the smaller 6⅜" soup and the 11¼" round platter. Dropped from the reissue were the oval platter, larger soup, sugar, creamer and tumblers.

According to an avid collector, the hardest to find pieces are the 8¼" vegetable bowl, tumblers and the 7¾" salad plate.

Bowl, 4⅞", dessert	4.00	Plate, 10", dinner	6.00
Bowl, 6⅜", soup	7.00	Platter, 11¼", round	10.00
Bowl, 8½", vegetable	12.00	Platter, 12", oval	10.00
Bowl, 8", rimmed soup	8.00	Saucer	1.00
Creamer	4.00	Sugar	3.00
Cup	3.00	Sugar lid	3.00
Plate, 7⅔", salad	3.00	Tumbler, 9 oz., ftd.	7.00
Plate, 9⅛", dinner	5.00	Tumbler, 10 oz., 5"	8.00

HARP JEANNETTE GLASS COMPANY, 1954-1957

Colors: crystal, crystal with gold trim, and cake stands in Shell Pink, pink, iridescent white and ice blue.

Harp cake stand varieties continue to be found! No wonder a collector can resort to collecting only Harp cake stands. There are enough different ones to keep you searching for a while. You can see two styles of ice blue, the ruffled, gold trim crystal and an iridescent one below. The Shell Pink Harp cake stand can be seen under that pattern. That brings the total to ten different cake stands in Harp. Thankfully, there are new additions turning up in this too small pattern. The ten varieties of cake stands are as follows:

- 1,2. Crystal with smooth or ruffled rim
- 3,4. Either of above with gold trim
- 5. Iridescent with smooth rim
- 6,7. White or Shell Pink (opaque) with beads on rim and foot
- 8,9. Ice blue with beads on foot and smooth or ruffled rim
- 10. Pink transparent

The Harp cake stand is reminiscent of early 1900's glassware. Most patterns after that time had cake plates instead of a stand.

Recently, cup and saucer prices have escalated. With so many new collectors starting on smaller sized patterns, the demand for basic pieces has raised the prices almost 75% in the last two years. There is not enough of this smaller pattern to accommodate everyone. The 7" plates may soon suffer the same fate as they are no more plentiful than the cup and saucers. Many collectors love this set to use for their bridge parties. With the cake stand, cups, saucers and the 7" plates, you can make a great small table setting.

As reported in the last book, the vase does stand 7½" and not 6" as it had previously been listed!

	Crystal		Crystal
Ash tray/coaster	5.00	Plate, 7"	10.00
Coaster	4.50	Saucer	6.50
Cup	13.50	**Tray, 2-handled, rectangular	32.50
*Cake stand, 9"	21.00	Vase, 7½"	20.00

* Ice blue, white, pink or Shell Pink - $30.00
** Shell Pink $50.00

HERITAGE FEDERAL GLASS COMPANY, 1940-1955

Colors: Crystal, some pink, blue, green and cobalt.

 Heritage prices have slowed down except for crystal creamers and 8½" berry bowls. These are still the most difficult of all pieces to find. The sugar turns up more frequently for some reason. I haven't seen one 8½" berry bowl for sale in the last year. Where did these bowls go? They used to be considered common! The reproduction berry bowls are so poorly made that they are causing little trouble for collectors. Why anyone would want to remake this little pattern is beyond my comprehension. Reproductions of Heritage bowls are being marketed by McCrory's, and other similar stores. These are being made in amber, crystal and green. Most are marked "MC" in the center. I say "most" because not all reports from readers have mentioned this mark. In any case, the smaller berry bowls are selling three for $1.00 and the larger for $1.59 each. The pattern on these pieces is not very good and should not fool even beginning collectors. Just compare the fully designed hobs in the photograph to the sparsely designed hobs on the reproductions. The green being found is much darker and closer to the avocado colored green of the 1970's than to the pretty shade of green shown here. Amber was never made originally; so that is no problem.

 Those pink, blue and green berry bowls all remain elusive. These are truly rare!

 Heritage was advertised as late as 1954 in some of the women's magazines.

 Crystal Heritage sets can be assembled more easily than sets of many other patterns due to the lack of different pieces. There are only ten separate pieces to find, so the limitation you have is whether to search for six, eight or twelve place settings. Thankfully, you only have to find one creamer and one large berry bowl no matter how many place settings you collect.

 Refer to Daisy for an explanation of Indiana's green Heritage pattern.

	Crystal	Pink	Blue Green
Bowl, 5", berry	8.00	40.00	50.00
Bowl, 8½", large berry	30.00	100.00	175.00
Bowl, 10½", fruit	13.50		
Cup	7.00		
Creamer, footed	22.50		
Plate, 8", luncheon	9.00		
Plate, 9¼", dinner	12.00		
Plate, 12", sandwich	13.00		
Saucer	4.00		
Sugar, open, footed	20.00		

HOLIDAY, "BUTTONS AND BOWS" JEANNETTE GLASS COMPANY, 1947-mid 1950's

Colors: Pink, iridescent; some Shell Pink and crystal.

 To reiterate, there are contrasting styles of Holiday pieces. Collectors need to be aware that there are three styles of cup and saucer sets. One style cup and saucer have a plain center. These are easy to match up and are shown on the left. There are two other styles of cups that have a rayed center. You can not mix these together since the base of the cup will not fit the saucer ring of the wrong type. Rayed cups have to go on rayed saucers, but you have to check these for size of the cup bottom also. One cup's base is 2" and fits a 2⅛" saucer ring. The other cup's base is 2⅜" and fits a 2½" saucer ring.

 There are two styles of 10 oz. tumblers, as can be seen in the picture. The tumbler on the right is flat bottomed, while the one on the left has a small raised foot and is narrower at the bottom. There is no difference in price, but purist collectors need to know that there are variances in pieces. These are just from different moulds, but new collectors sometimes get upset with differences on the same item purchased in different places.

 While we are pointing out differences, there are also two style sherbets. The one on the right has a rayed foot while the one on the left is plain. The two sherbet plates both have 2¾" centers, but the one on the left has a "beads" effect in the center while the one on the right has a center ring with a "diamond" effect in the center. These mould variations occur in many patterns, but it is confusing unless you know what to expect. It is all right to mix styles, but some people do not wish to do so. These confusing items are all shown on the bottom of page 101.

HOLIDAY, "BUTTONS AND BOWS" JEANNETTE GLASS COMPANY, 1947-mid 1950's (Cont.)

If you missed page 100, be sure to refer to it to learn about the different styles of Holiday pieces.

It has become apparent that Holiday suffered the same fate as Floral and Doric and Pansy. The pieces we have difficulty in finding in these patterns were exported. Unlike the other patterns that seem to have been sent to England, Holiday was exported to the Philippines. As reported in the ninth *Collector's Encyclopedia of Depression Glass*, iced teas, soups and juices have been found in abundance there. The tumblers were sent in boxes of six to be used as premiums for buying Hershey's chocolate bars. As a footnote, now that the Philippines have been deserted by the Armed Forces, I doubt that there will be any significant quantities of these pieces ever imported from there again. A few "in the know" service personnel were gathering these items while stationed there!

I omitted the 10½" iridescent sandwich tray from the price listing last time. This happens when you have never priced a color that has only a few pieces in that pattern. I did list three out of four!

Holiday console bowls, candlesticks and cake plates are the most difficult pieces to find outside of those pieces that were exported. If you wonder how such a lately manufactured glassware could have so many hard to find pieces, welcome to the club. Evidently, there was little demand for pieces other than the basics. Maybe the serving pieces were premiums. No data has ever surfaced to **explain** these mysteries. Holiday seems to have been a heavily used pattern judging by the multitude of damaged pieces I have examined as I have looked at sets over the years. Those pointed edges did not hold up well to banging and bumping. They still do not as many glass dealers will attest!

You should also be aware in examining Holiday that the points that protrude are prone to chips, nicks and "chigger bites," an auction term that varies from place to place. Some auction houses must harbor some big chiggers! Remember, damaged glass can not be "almost" mint. The prices listed here are for **mint** condition glassware!

	Pink	Crystal	Iridescent
Bowl, 5⅛", berry	12.00		
Bowl, 7¾", soup	45.00		
Bowl, 8½", large berry	24.00		
Bowl, 9½", oval vegetable	24.00		
*Bowl, 10¾", console	100.00		
Butter dish and cover	37.50		
Butter dish bottom	10.00		
Butter dish top	27.50		
Cake plate, 10½", 3 legged	85.00		
Candlesticks, 3" pr.	85.00		
Creamer, footed	8.00		
Cup, three sizes	7.00		
Pitcher, 4¾", 16 oz. milk	55.00	15.00	20.00
Pitcher, 6¾", 52 oz.	35.00		
Plate, 6", sherbet	6.00		
Plate, 9", dinner	16.00		
Plate, 13¾", chop	85.00		
Platter, 11⅜", oval	20.00		12.50
Sandwich tray, 10½"	17.50		15.00
Saucer, 3 styles	6.00		
Sherbet, 2 styles	6.00		
Sugar	10.00		
Sugar cover	15.00		
Tumbler, 4", 10 oz., flat	19.00		
Tumbler, 4", footed, 5 oz.	37.50		10.00
Tumbler, 4¼", footed, 5¼ oz.		7.50	
Tumbler, 6", footed	130.00		

* Shell Pink $40.00

Please refer to Foreword for pricing information

IRIS, "IRIS AND HERRINGBONE" JEANNETTE GLASS COMPANY, 1928-1932; 1950's; 1970's

Colors: Crystal, iridescent; some pink; recently bi-colored red/yellow and blue/green combinations and white.

Iris became one of the more difficult patterns to place in this division between *The Collector's Encyclopedia of Depression Glass* and *Collectible Glassware from the 40's, 50's, 60's ...* since it fits both time periods so well. Iridescent Iris belongs entirely within the frame of this book, and although crystal production goes back to 1928 for its start, some crystal was made in the late 1940's, 1950's; and some pieces, such as candy bottoms and vases, were manufactured as late as the early 1970's. Thus, I have decided to include crystal prices here also.

Realize those candy bottoms in iridescent are a product of the 1970's when Jeannette made crystal bottoms and flashed them with two-tone colors such as red/yellow or blue/green. Many of these were sold as vases and, over time, the colors have washed or peeled off making crystal candy bottoms. These can be distinguished by the lack of rays on the foot of the dish. The later made ones all are plain footed. Similarly, white vases were made and sprayed green, red and blue on the outside. Many of these vases have lost the colors on the outside and are now only white. White vases of this vintage sell in the $8.00-10.00 range.

As I write this in March, I can say that the question raised most often this last year is, "When are the prices for Iris going to stop going up?" If I knew that, I would be rich, and I'd be fishing! I would have bought all those pieces that I thought were over priced two years ago and doubled my money. I said that Iris was the hottest selling crystal pattern in my ninth *Collector's Encyclopedia of Depression Glass*, but little did I realize what an understatement that was! It was only beginning to be **HOT!**

About the time that book came out with Iris on the cover, everyone seemed to want to collect it. There was already a short supply of many pieces because of the heavy demand from the South, Tennessee in particular, where Iris is the state flower. Suddenly, no dealer could have enough stock of this pattern, and the demand far out stripped the supply. A few dealers began to raise prices, and suddenly the race was on to see who could get the highest prices. Many collectors got caught up in the frenzy, and some prices, almost doubled. Now, those prices have almost doubled again on the harder to find pieces.

The water goblet and the demitasse cup and saucer are the most difficult pieces to find in the iridescent color.

The decorated red and gold Iris that keeps turning up was called "Corsage" and styled by Century in 1946. We know this because of a card attached to a 1946 "Corsage" wedding gift that a reader shared with me. Does anyone know more?

The bowls advertising "Badcock Furniture will treat you right" are coming from the southern part of the country. When I asked about Badcock Furniture in my last book, I had only been living in Florida a short while and was not familiar with this **large** chain of furniture stores. Cathy always said I never noticed furniture. I guess that proves her right! I found them out from an advertising circular that came in the mail, but it was too late to change it in my writing. In any case, thanks, readers, for all the calls, letters, explanations at shows, mailing envelopes from the stores, yellow page listings, names of sales personnel and even a recent advertising mug from Badcock Furniture! I wonder if Badcock knows how well it is known nationally! Thanks, too, for really **reading** the book!

	Crystal	Iridescent	Green/ Pink		Crystal	Iridescent	Green/ Pink
Bowl, 4½", berry, beaded edge	38.00	9.00		Goblet, 4¼", 4 oz., cocktail	24.00		
Bowl, 5", ruffled, sauce	9.00	24.00		Goblet, 4¼", 3 oz., wine	16.00		
Bowl, 5", cereal	100.00			Goblet, 5¾", 4 oz.	24.00		
Bowl, 7½", soup	145.00	55.00		Goblet, 5¾", 8 oz.	24.00	150.00	
Bowl, 8", berry, beaded edge	75.00	20.00		**Lamp shade, 11½"	85.00		
Bowl, 9½", ruffled, salad	12.50	13.00	95.00	Pitcher, 9½", footed	37.50	40.00	
Bowl, 11½", ruffled, fruit	15.00	14.00		Plate, 5½", sherbet	14.00	13.00	
Bowl, 11", fruit, straight edge	50.00			Plate, 8", luncheon	95.00		
Butter dish and cover	47.50	40.00		Plate, 9", dinner	50.00	37.50	
Butter dish bottom	13.50	12.00		Plate, 11¾", sandwich	30.00	30.00	
Butter dish top	34.00	28.50		Saucer	12.00	11.00	
Candlesticks, pr.	40.00	42.50		Sherbet, 2½", footed	24.00	14.00	
Candy jar and cover	125.00			Sherbet, 4", footed	20.00		
Coaster	90.00			Sugar	11.00	11.00	100.00
Creamer, footed	11.00	12.00	100.00	Sugar cover	12.00	12.00	
Cup	15.00	14.00		Tumbler, 4", flat	120.00		
*Demitasse cup	35.00	115.00		Tumbler, 6", footed	18.00	16.00	
*Demitasse saucer	130.00	150.00		Tumbler, 6½", footed	32.00		
Fruit or nut set	60.00			Vase, 9"	27.50	24.00	125.00
Goblet, 4", wine		30.00					

*Ruby, Blue, Amethyst priced as Iridescent
**Colors: $65.00

Please refer to Foreword for pricing information

JAMESTOWN FOSTORIA GLASS COMPANY, 1958-1982

Colors: Amber, amethyst, blue, brown, crystal, green, pink and red.

Jamestown is another of those patterns where stemware seems to be all that is available to buy. Serving pieces were not marketed by Fostoria for as long as the stemware was, so that means that collectors and dealers alike are now searching for serving pieces! Not all pieces were made in each color. I have grouped the colors into three pricing groups. Many dealers do not stock the amber or brown. They have found that there is little demand for these colors at present. If you are looking for amber or brown, ask dealers for it. You should be able to find some bargains. In the middle group, crystal is most in demand. Ruby sells almost as fast as crystal, but there is not a complete line of the Ruby. Many hostesses want the Ruby goblets for Christmas table settings.

As I pointed out previously, the line numbers on the same stems have two different sizes and capacities listed for the same item. These listings came from two separate Fostoria catalogues, and it is one of the many things that drives me to distraction when writing a book. Which figure do you use? Thus, I have included both stem listings for the purist. Either someone measured incorrectly one year or the sizes were actually changed. If you have pieces with both measurements, please let me know! I have run into this in other company's catalogues, so I point this out to make you aware of why your measurements could differ from those I have listed.

	Amber/Brown	Amethyst/Crystal/Green	Blue/Pink/Ruby
Bowl, 4½", dessert #2719/421	8.50	13.50	16.00
Bowl, 10", salad #2719//211	21.00	37.50	42.50
Bowl, 10", two hndl. serving #2719/648	21.00	40.00	50.00
Butter w/cover, ¼ pound #2719/300	24.00	45.00	55.00
Cake plate, 9½", hndl. #2719/306	16.00	32.50	37.50
Celery, 9¼" #2719/360	18.00	32.50	37.50
Cream, 3½", ftd. #2719/681	11.00	16.00	24.00
Jelly w/cover, 6⅛" #2719/447	32.50	55.00	75.00
Pickle, 8⅜" #2719/540	21.00	35.00	40.00
Pitcher, 7⁵⁄₁₆", 48 oz., ice jug #2719/456	45.00	90.00	120.00
Plate, 8" #2719/550	8.50	16.00	19.00
Plate, 14", torte #2719/567	26.00	42.50	55.00
Relish, 9⅛", 2 part #2719/620	16.00	32.00	37.50
Salad set, 4 pc. (10" bowl, 14" plate w/wood fork & spoon) #2719/286	55.00	85.00	100.00
Salver, 7" high, 10" diameter #2719/630	55.00	100.00	100.00
Sauce dish w/cover, 4½" #2719/635	18.00	30.00	34.00
Shaker, 3½", w/chrome top. pr. #2719/653	26.00	37.50	47.50
Stem, 4⁵⁄₁₆", 4 oz., wine #2719/26	10.00	20.00	24.00
Stem, 4¼", 6½ oz., sherbet #2719/7	6.50	12.50	17.50
Stem, 4⅛", 7 oz., sherbet #2719/7	6.50	12.50	17.50
Stem, 5¾", 9½ oz., goblet #2719/2	10.00	20.00	20.50
Stem, 5⅞", 10 oz., goblet #2719/2	10.00	20.00	20.50
Sugar, 3½", ftd. #2719/679	11.00	17.50	24.00
Tray, 9⅜", hndl. muffin #2719/726	26.00	42.50	55.00
Tumbler, 4¼", 9 oz. #2719/73	9.00	21.00	25.00
Tumbler, 4¾", 5 oz., juice #2719/88	9.50	21.00	26.00
Tumbler, 5⅛", 12 oz. #2719/64	9.00	21.00	26.00
Tumbler, 6", 11 oz., ftd. tea #2719/63	10.00	21.00	24.00
Tumbler, 6", 12 oz., ftd. tea #2719/63	10.00	21.00	24.00

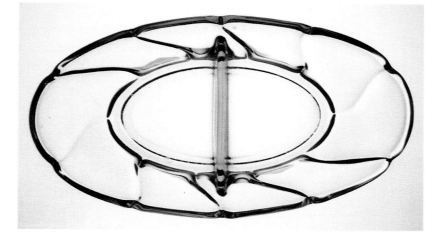

KING'S CROWN THUMBPRINT LINE No. 4016 U.S. GLASS (TIFFIN) COMPANY, LATE 1800'S - 1960'S; INDIANA GLASS COMPANY, 1970'S

Colors: Crystal, crystal with ruby or cranberry flash, crystal with gold or platinum.

King's Crown is a pattern that causes some confusion among both old and new collectors. Originally issued as Thumbprint Line No. 4016 by U. S. Glass in the late 1800's, this glassware was also made by Tiffin into the early 1960's. The catalogue reprint shown in this section is from 1955. To make matters more problematical, Indiana bought the moulds and changed the design somewhat.

For this book I am including the Indiana pieces as well as those made by Tiffin after 1940. You may find additional pieces, but please realize that many of those could be from an earlier time. Some pieces are flashed with gold, platinum, green, yellow, cranberry or the ruby. For now, until a market is more clearly established, there will be no price distinction on the different flashed colors. Subtract twenty-five to forty percent of the prices listed for crystal. Gold and platinum decorated products were also made at Indiana. Furthermore, iridized Carnival colors, Avocado green, amber and other solid colored items were made by Indiana.

The elongated thumbprint designs were the original moulds. Some of this elongated style may have been made at Indiana before they changed the moulds, but if the pieces you have show circular thumbprints, you have King's Crown made by Indiana. Also, the Tiffin tumblers are flared at the top while Indiana's are straight. Expect to pay about half the prices below for the more recently issued Indiana tumblers.

	Ruby Flashed		Ruby Flashed
Ash tray, 5¼", square	10.00	Plate, 7⅜", mayonnaise liner	12.50
Bowl, 4", finger	15.00	Plate, 7⅜", salad	12.00
Bowl, 4", mayonnaise	15.00	Plate, 9¾", snack w/indent	15.00
Bowl, 6", diameter, ftd., wedding or candy	25.00	Plate, 10", dinner	30.00
Bowl, 8¾", 2-hdld., crimped bon bon	35.00	Plate, 14½", torte	40.00
Bowl, 9¼", salad	45.00	Plate, 24", party	60.00
Bowl, 10½", ftd., wedding or candy, w/cover	65.00	Plate, 24", party server (w/punch ft.)	95.00
Bowl, 11½", 4½" high, crimped	55.00	Punch bowl foot	35.00
Bowl, 11¼" cone	40.00	Punch bowl, 2 styles	150.00
Bowl, 12½", center edge, 3" high	35.00	Punch cup	8.00
Bowl, 12½", flower floater	35.00	Punch set, 15 pc. w/foot	300.00
Bowl, crimped, ftd.	25.00	Punch set, 15 pc. w/plate	325.00
Bowl, flared, ftd.	36.00	Relish, 14", 5 part	55.00
Bowl, straight edge	40.00	Saucer	7.00
Cake salver, 12½", ftd.	60.00	Stem, 2 oz., wine	7.50
Candleholder, sherbet type	22.50	Stem, 2¼ oz., cocktail	12.50
Candleholder, 2-lite, 5½"	25.00	Stem, 4 oz., claret	12.00
Candy box, 6", flat, w/cover	32.00	Stem, 4 oz., oyster cocktail	12.50
Cheese stand	15.00	Stem, 5½ oz., sundae or sherbet	10.00
Compote, 7¼", 9¾" diameter	25.00	Stem, 9 oz., water goblet	12.00
Compote, 7½", 12" diameter, ftd., crimped	55.00	Sugar	20.00
Compote, small, flat	15.00	Tumbler, 4 oz., juice, ftd.	10.00
Creamer	20.00	Tumbler, 4½ oz., juice	12.00
Cup	8.00	Tumbler, 8½ oz., water	12.00
Lazy susan, 24", 8½" high, w/ball bearing spinner	100.00	Tumbler, 11 oz., ice tea	15.00
Mayonnaise, 3 pc. set	25.00	Tumbler, 12 oz., ice tea, ftd.	17.50
Pitcher	100.00	Vase, 9", bud	25.00
Plate, 5", bread/butter	8.00	Vase, 12¼", bud	40.00

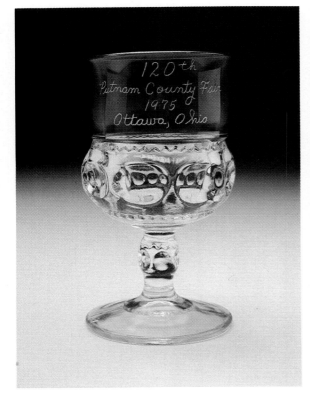

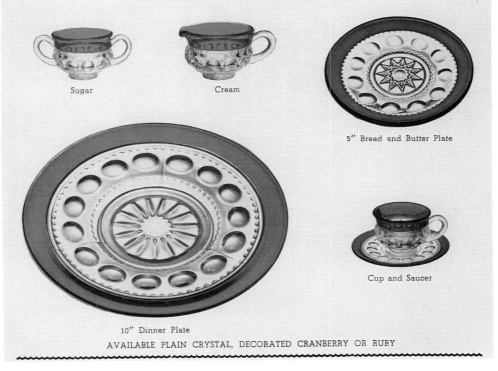

United States Glass Company
TIFFIN, OHIO

KINGS CROWN
Also known as No. 4016 Thumbprint

Sugar

Cream

5" Bread and Butter Plate

10" Dinner Plate

Cup and Saucer

AVAILABLE PLAIN CRYSTAL, DECORATED CRANBERRY OR RUBY

Center Edge Bowl 12½" Diameter 3" High

2-Lite Candle Holder 5½" High

Footed Fruit Compote 9¾" Diameter 7¼" High

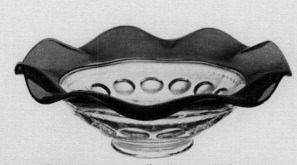

Crimped Bowl 11½" Diameter 4½" High

Cone Bowl 11¼" Diameter 4¾" High

Goblet 9 oz.

Wine 2 oz.

Juice 4 oz.

Claret 4 oz.

Cocktail 2¼ oz.

Oyster Cocktail 4 oz.

Sundae 5½ oz.

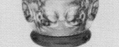

Water Tumbler 8½ oz.

Juice Tumbler 4½ oz.

Footed Ice Tea 12 oz.   Ice Tea Tumbler 11 oz.

Finger Bowl 4″ Diameter

7⅜″ Salad Plate

AVAILABLE PLAIN CRYSTAL, DECORATED CRANBERRY OR RUBY   Page 3

KINGS CROWN

15 pc. Punch Set, with foot
Capacity 12 qts. Diameter 23"

15 pc. Punch Set Flared
Capacity 12 qts. Plate Diameter 23"

Party Server 24" Diameter 8" High

AVAILABLE PLAIN CRYSTAL, DECORATED CRANBERRY OR RUBY

KINGS
CROWN

Wedding Bowl and Cover
6" Diameter 10½" High

Flower Floater 12½" Diameter

Torte Plate 14" Diameter

Ash Tray 5¼" Square

Footed Cake Salver
12½" Diameter 4¾" High

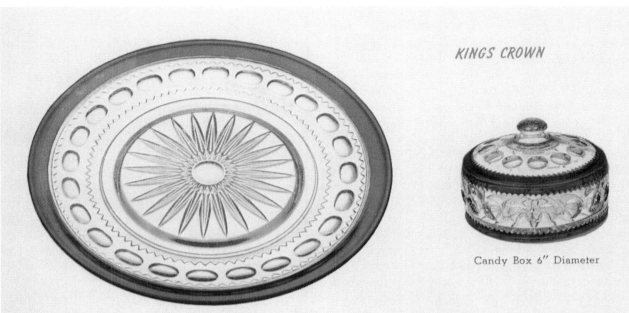

24" Party Plate

KINGS CROWN

Candy Box 6" Diameter

Lazy Susan 24" Diameter 8½" High Complete with Ballbearing Spinner

5 Part Relish 14" Diameter

3 pc. Mayonnaise Set. Plate 7-⅜" Bowl 4"

MODERNTONE PLATONITE
HAZEL ATLAS GLASS COMPANY, 1940-early 1950's

Colors: Platonite pastel, white and white decorated.

Searching for pieces of Platonite Moderntone not shown in the first *Collectible Glassware from the 40's, 50's, 60's ...* became a real challenge as I worked on this new book. I have changed a few photographs, this time, but I will do a major overhaul in the third book. The organization of colors was set up to show the varieties available and not necessarily to help me in pricing. Because there are varying shades that make differences in price, I chose color as the predominate factor in laying out the photographs. Children's dishes have their own section starting on page 122.

There is still little demand for the plain white; but a few collectors are beginning to notice the white trimmed in red, et cetera. Exhibit a piece of Blue or Red Willow or Deco trimmed Moderntone (shown on page 117) and you will see collectors' eyes light up! I have seen very little of the Willow decorated Moderntone, but it is striking on the Platonite white! All the Deco decorated pieces in the top photograph came out of one set found by an Ohio dealer years ago.

Pastel colors are the lighter shades of blue, green, pink and yellow.

You may notice that there are two distinct shades of pink on the bottom of page 119. I have been assured by Moderntone collectors that this difference in shade is of no consequence to them. It bothers me to the point that I placed the lighter shades on the far right of the photograph to illustrate my point regarding color shades. The printing of the book did a good job of making both shades of pink look the same in the first edition! We will hope for better results here.

Since my Mom and a local collector are trying to obtain the world's largest accumulation of Moderntone, observations expressed here have come from the gathering of at least 3,500 pieces of Platonite and over 1,500 pieces of children's sets. That is an adequate representation to show a few trends about availability and rarity.

In pastel colors, there remains little price difference on the pieces with white interiors as opposed to those with colored interiors. My sales records show that the colored interiors are faster sellers. My wife, however, prefers the white interiors. I believe the colored interiors are in lesser supply.

All bowls come with or without rims. Bowls without rims are more difficult to find, but bowls with rims also tend to have more inner rim roughness which "turns off" many collectors. Pastel pink 8" bowls with or without rims and yellow 12" platters are easier to find than other pastel colors. These may have been a premium at one time that would make their abundance believable.

For observations about the darker colors of Platonite, turn to page 120.

	Pastel Colors	White or w/stripes	Deco/Red or Blue Willow
Bowl, 4¾", cream soup	6.50	4.00	17.50
Bowl, 5", berry, w/rim	5.00	3.00	11.00
Bowl, 5", berry, wo/rim	6.00		
Bowl, 5", deep cereal, w/white	7.50	4.00	
Bowl, 5", deep cereal, wo/white	9.00		
Bowl, 8", w/rim	*12.50	6.00	25.00
Bowl, 8", wo/rim	*17.50		
Bowl, 8¾", large berry		7.00	26.00
Creamer	5.00	4.00	17.50
Cup	3.50	2.50	20.00
Mug, 4", 8 oz.		8.00	
Plate, 6¾", sherbet	4.50	2.50	9.00
Plate, 8⅞", dinner	6.50	3.50	20.00
Plate, 10½", sandwich	15.00	8.00	
Platter, 11", oval		12.50	25.00
Platter, 12", oval	**14.00	9.00	27.50
Salt and pepper, pr.	16.00	13.00	
Saucer	2.00	1.50	4.00
Sherbet	4.50	2.50	11.00
Sugar	5.00	4.00	17.00
Tumbler, 9 oz.	9.00		
Tumbler, cone, ftd.		6.00	

*Pink $8.50
* *Yellow $8.00

Please refer to Foreword for pricing information

MODERNTONE PLATONITE (Cont.)
HAZEL ATLAS GLASS COMPANY, 1940-early 1950's

Colors: Dark Platonite fired-on colors.

Collecting pastel Platonite will give you a few problems in finding some of the pieces, but collecting the darker or later colors will test your patience! There is so little of the darker colors available compared to the quantities of the pastel, you should be prepared to buy it whenever you see it!

My price list below divides colors into two distinct price groups based upon availability. The first group consists of cobalt blue, turquoise green, "lemon" yellow and orange. These can be found pictured as: cobalt (top page 121 left), turquoise (top page 118 left), "lemon" (top page 119 left) and orange (bottom page 119). All of these colors can be collected in sets with difficulty, but they can be found eventually. All can be found with white or colored interiors. White interiors are more plentiful, but it only matters if you do not wish to mix the different color treatments made by Hazel Atlas.

Accumulating a set of any of the other colors, i.e., Chartreuse, Burgundy, Green, Gray, "rust" or "gold" is another matter. As far as I can determine, none of the preceding colors can be found with white interiors. These colors are shown at the top of page 122 except for Chartreuse that can only be seen in the child's set on the left at the bottom of page 124. The sugar, creamer and cup are Chartreuse in that set. Colors shown on the top of page 122 are as follows: Burgundy, Green, Gray, "rust" and "gold." Collectors have called the Green incorrectly "forest green" and the Burgundy "maroon." I have also heard the "gold" referred to as "butterscotch" which is a better name as far as I am concerned. As with the pink, some collectors may consider the "gold" merely a variation of the "lemon" yellow and not a separate color.

In any case, you have a challenge on your hands if you pick any of the aforementioned colors to collect! Note that several pieces are not listed in my prices. So far, cream soups, bowls with rims, sandwich plates and salt and pepper shakers have not been found in any of these colors! Green (dark) tumblers seem to be the color most often found in these later colors.

Shown at the bottom of page 121 is a cone shaped tumbler only found in white. The lid has been photographed so you can see how this tumbler was given free with the purchase of "Lovely" cherry gelatin for 10¢. Many tumblers were obtained during this era by acquiring a product.

	Cobalt/Turquoise Lemon/Orange	Burgundy/Chartreuse Green/Gray/Rust/Gold
Bowl, 4¾", cream soup	10.00	
Bowl, 5", berry, w/rim	11.00	
Bowl, 5", berry, wo/rim	8.00	11.00
Bowl, 5", deep cereal, w/white	110.00	
Bowl, 5", deep cereal, wo/white		14.00
Bowl, 8", w/rim	27.50	
Bowl, 8", wo/rim	27.50	32.50
Creamer	8.00	10.00
Cup	6.00	7.00
Plate, 6¾", sherbet	6.00	8.00
Plate, 8⅞" dinner	11.00	12.00
Plate, 10½" sandwich	20.00	
Platter, 12" oval	20.00	27.50
Salt and pepper, pr.	22.50	
Saucer	5.00	6.00
Sherbet	7.00	9.00
Sugar	8.00	10.00
Tumbler, 9 oz.	12.50	22.50

MODERNTONE "LITTLE HOSTESS PARTY DISHES"
HAZEL ATLAS GLASS COMPANY, early 1950's

LITTLE HOSTESS PARTY DISHES have caught the eye of doll collectors and doll dish collectors. This causes prices to rise even more because there are collectors from other venues searching for these little sets.

As a child, my wife received a set as a gift premium from Big Top Peanut Butter. (See top page 124.)

You will note price increases in the harder to find colors. An all white set has been found in an original box. It is photographed for use in the next book. Turquoise teapots remain more difficult to find than the Burgundy. A problem occurs in matching the shades of Burgundy when buying this teapot top and bottom separately. If you do not have one piece with you when you buy the other, I would suggest refraining from doing so unless the price is very reasonable.

Notice that the child's cups were also sold as souvenir items. This particular one shown with the pink and black is from Canada.

LITTLE HOSTESS PARTY SET
Pink/Black/White (top 123)

Cup, ¾", bright pink, white	15.00
Saucer, 3⅞", black, white	12.00
Plate, 5¼", black, bright pink, white	15.00
Creamer, 1¾", bright pink	17.50
Sugar, 1¾", bright pink	17.50
Teapot, 3½", bright pink	70.00
Teapot lid, black	70.00
Set, 16 piece	335.00

LITTLE HOSTESS PARTY SET
Lemon/Beige/Pink/Aqua
(bottom 123)

Cup, ¾", bright pink/aqua/lemon	15.00
Saucer, 3⅞", same	12.00
Plate, 5¼", same	15.00
Creamer, 1¾", pink	17.50
Sugar, 1¾", pink	17.50
Teapot, 3½", brown	70.00

Teapot lid, lemon	70.00
Set, 16 piece	335.00

LITTLE HOSTESS PARTY SET
Gray/Rust/Gold
Turquoise (top 124)

Cup, ¾", Gray, rust	12.00
Cup, ¾", gold, turquoise	12.00
Saucer, 3⅞", all four colors	8.00
Plate, 5¼", same	8.00
Creamer, 1¾", rust	12.50
Sugar, 1¾", rust	12.50
Teapot, 3½", turquoise	62.50
Teapot lid, turquoise	62.50
Set, 16 piece	275.00

LITTLE HOSTESS PARTY SET
Green/Gray/Chartreuse/
Burgundy (bottom 124 left)

Cup, ¾", Green, Gray, Chartreuse	10.00

Cup, ¾", Burgundy	12.00
Saucer, 3⅞", Green, Gray & Burgundy, Chartreuse	7.00
Plate, 5¼", Burgundy	10.00
Plate, 5¼", Green, Gray, Chartreuse	8.00
Creamer, 1¾", Chartreuse	12.50
Sugar, 1¾", Chartreuse	12.50
Teapot, 3½", Burgundy	50.00
Teapot lid, Burgundy	55.00
Set, 16 piece	235.00

LITTLE HOSTESS PARTY SET
Pastel pink/green/blue
yellow (bottom 124 right)

Cup, ¾", all four colors	9.00
Saucer, 3⅞", same	7.00
Plate, 5¼", same	10.00
Creamer, 1¾", pink	12.50
Sugar, 1¾", pink	12.50
Set, 14 piece	105.00

Please refer to Foreword for pricing information

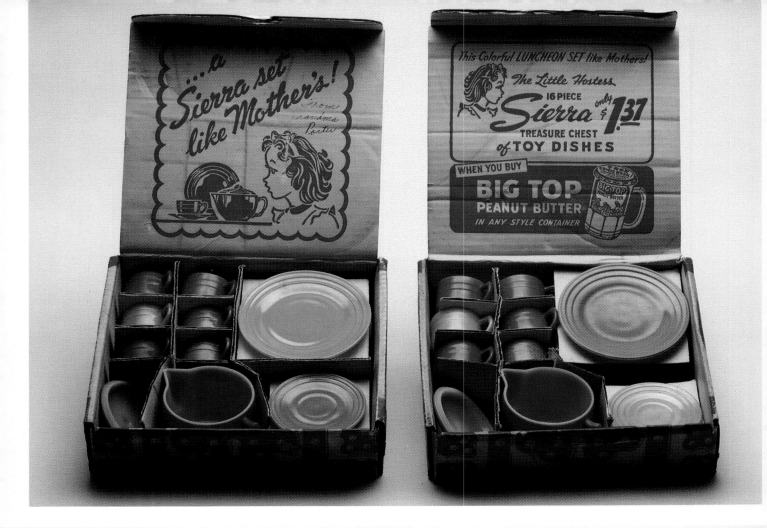

MOONSTONE ANCHOR HOCKING GLASS CORPORATION, 1941-1946

Colors: crystal with opalescent hobnails and some green with opalescent hobnails.

Originally, Moonstone was the dividing pattern between *The Collector's Encyclopedia of Depression Glass* and this book. Unfortunately, there are some patterns with rather vague dates of manufacture and some overlapping time periods that do not make the dividing line of 1940 quite as exacting as I would have liked. In any case, Moonstone is truly 1940's glassware and I hope you enjoy seeing the original photograph of a J. J. Newberry store window display on page 127 one last time. Thanks for all the letters I received from readers who enjoyed seeing these original photographs. No, I do not have others besides the ones I have shown before; but I wish I did.

The 5½" berry bowl shown in the foreground on the right of page 126 and listed as M2775 in the Hocking brochure is the most difficult piece to find today. There are none of those in the store display photo either! Goblets, cups and saucers are also missing in that store window display, and they are easily found today. The ruffled 5½" bowls are more readily found, but even they are not abundant. Have you noticed that all sizes of plates have disappeared into collections? I might point out that the measurement on the luncheon plate is exactly 8⅜" and the sandwich plate measures 10¾" instead of 10" as I have previously listed.

The green colored ware was issued under the name "Ocean Green" and was made in sets containing goblets, cups, saucers, plates, creamer and sugars. Notice the two pieces shown are slightly different from the standard line in the catalogue pages on 126. I wonder if the pink shown in bottom photograph had a name. This photograph was furnished by Anchor Hocking of Moonstone pieces found in their morgue. Discontinued or experimental items were sometimes stored in some room or place appropriately called a morgue.

Moonstone collectors buy Fenton Hobnail pitchers and tumblers to go with their sets since there are no pitchers or tumblers in Moonstone.

There are no Moonstone shakers. Those found are Fenton. There is no Moonstone cologne bottle. It, also, is Fenton. The Fenton pieces go well with Moonstone; and, if you would like additional pieces that are similar to your pattern, of course buy these! The hobs on the Fenton are more pointed than on Moonstone, but the colors match very well.

	Opalescent Hobnail		Opalescent Hobnail
Bowl, 5½", berry	16.00	Cup	8.00
Bowl, 5½", crimped, dessert	9.50	Goblet, 10 oz.	18.00
Bowl, 6½", crimped, handled	10.00	Heart bonbon, one handle	12.00
Bowl, 7¾", flat	12.00	Plate, 6¼", sherbet	6.50
Bowl, 7¾", divided relish	11.00	Plate, 8⅜", luncheon	15.00
Bowl, 9½", crimped	20.00	Plate, 10¾", sandwich	25.00
Bowl, cloverleaf	12.50	Puff box and cover, 4¾", round	22.50
Candle holder, pr.	17.50	Saucer (same as sherbet plate)	6.50
Candy jar and cover, 6"	25.00	Sherbet, footed	7.00
Cigarette jar and cover	22.50	Sugar, footed	9.00
Creamer	9.00	Vase, 5½", bud	12.00

Please refer to Foreword for pricing information

Opalescent "MOONSTONE" Glassware

"MOONSTONE" Glassware

	DOZ. TO CTN.	WT. OF CTN.
Tableware		
M2779— 3⅞" Cup	6	32#
M2729— 6¼" Saucer	6	32#
M2713— 6 oz. Sherbet	6	32#
M2729— 6¼" Sherbet Plate	6	32#
M2775— 5½" Dessert	6	32#
M2716— 10 oz. Goblet	4	36#
M2740— 8⅜" Luncheon Plate	4	44#
Gift Ware		
M2769— 7¾" Divided Relish	2	27#
M2766— 6½" Crimped Handled Bowl	2	19#
M2755— 6¾" Clover Leaf Dish	2	23#
M2772— 6½" Heart Bonbon	2	20#
M2767— 7¾" Flat Bowl	2	23#
M2753— 3¼" Sugar	2	13#
M2754— 3¼" Creamer	2	12½#
M2722— 4¾" Puff Box & Cover	2	22#
M2799— 5" Cigarette Jar & Cover	2	25#
M2782— 5½" Vase	2	16#
M2792— 6" Candy Jar & Cover	1	20#
M2760— 10¾" Sandwich Plate	1	21#
M2768— 9½" Crimped Bowl	1	21#
M2765— 5½" Crimped Dessert	6	33#
M2781— 4¼" Candleholder	2	10#
Suggested Sets - Bulk Packed		
M2700/1—7 Pce. Dessert Set (Bulk Packed in 2 Cartons)	12 Sets	54#
M2700/2—4 Pce. Buffet Set (Bulk Packed in 3 Cartons)	12 Sets	52#

Now Available at Low Prices

MOROCCAN AMETHYST HAZEL WARE, DIVISION OF CONTINENTAL CAN, 1960's

Color: Amethyst.

Moroccan Amethyst is the **color** that is found on several styles and shapes of this Hazel Ware glass. Like Anchor Hocking's Forest Green and Royal Ruby, the color was more important than the shape of the pieces. Thus, pattern took second place to color with Hazel Atlas as it did for Anchor Hocking!

As you can see by the expanded listing, many new pieces are still being found. One of the more interesting is the salad bowl set found at a flea market south of Pittsburgh last summer. You can see the large and smaller apple shaped bowls on the top of page 129. These pieces have an embossed apple blossom design in the bottom. There is also a floral design in the bottom of the 4½" square ash tray, but it is obliterated by the original Moroccan Amethyst sticker. The 4½", five pointed star candlesticks were an additional find with this purchase. All these items came from the family of a worker at the Hazel Atlas plant. The seller promised me more pieces the following month, so I went all the way back to see what else was available. Unfortunately, he did not attend that month as he promised.

The bottom of page 129 shows other colors being found. You will find swirled bowls in green, amber and white! They are usually priced reasonably in these colors and I suspect that they are later productions made to go with the 1970's Avocado and Harvest Gold colors prevalent then. Crystal and white goblets are also being found. Look under Capri (page 22) for a discussion of the crystal.

I have an original box for the amethyst and white punch bowl set that calls this Alpine. Notice that the punch cups have open handles to hang onto the side of the punch bowl. I have seen some wild prices on this set, but I was able to attain mine for $75.00 by the time I found four missing cups. I also saw a "Seashell" snack set in the same two colors, and it was also identified as "Alpine." I wasn't wild about the price; so I do not own it! The punch sets are selling in the $100.00 range.

The **four** stemmed pieces shown on the top of page 131 have all been found with Moroccan Amethyst labels; so there is no question as to their inclusion in our list. There may be another size in this design. I have not found any other sizes of crinkled design tumblers other than the 11 oz.; but a friend lent me a juice and an iced tea that you can see at the top of page 130. All the pieces shown in that picture were borrowed including the four-part lazy susan or relish consisting of four 7¾" oval bowls in a metal holder. One of the fun things about collecting a pattern for which I have not found a catalogue listing is finding new pieces not listed! Send me a picture and measurements of what **you** discover!

"The Magic Hour" 4 pc. cocktail set on page 133 features a clock showing six o'clock and says "yours" on one side and "mine" on the other. In this boxed set are two, 2½", 4 oz. tumblers and a spouted cocktail with glass stirrer to make up the four pieces. You will find two and three tier tidbit trays made out of many different pieces in this pattern including bowls, plates and ash trays.

The 7¾" bowl on the bottom right of page 130 is the only piece of this pattern that I have seen with an acid etched design although the dealer who sold it to me said she had found two! Not much of the sprayed on red over crystal is being found, but there is also little demand for it at present. The crystal, amber and green pieces may someday be desirable to own; but for now, that does not seem to be the case!

	Amethyst		Amethyst
Ash tray, 3¼", triangular	5.50	Goblet, 4¼", 7½ oz., sherbet	7.50
Ash tray, 3¼", round	5.50	Goblet, 4⅜", 5½ oz., juice	9.00
Ash tray, 6⅞", triangular	9.50	Goblet, 5½", 9 oz., water	10.00
Ash tray, 8", square	13.00	Ice bucket, 6"	30.00
Bowl, 4¾", fruit, octagonal	6.50	Plate, 5¾"	4.50
Bowl, 5¾", deep, square	10.00	Plate, 7¼", salad	7.00
Bowl, 6", round	11.00	Plate, 9¾", dinner	9.00
Bowl, 7¾", oval	16.00	Plate, 10", fan shaped, snack w/cup rest	8.00
Bowl. 7¾", rectangular	14.00	Plate, 12", sandwich, w/metal /handle	12.50
Bowl. 7¾", rectangular w/ metal handle	16.00	Saucer	1.00
Bowl, 10¾"	27.50	Tumbler, 4 oz., juice, 2½"	8.50
Candy w/lid short	30.00	Tumbler, 8 oz., old fashion, 3¼"	14.00
Candy w/lid tall	30.00	Tumbler, 9 oz., water	10.00
Chip and dip, 10¾" & 5¾" bowls in metal holder	37.50	Tumbler, 11 oz., water, crinkled bottom, 4¼"	12.00
Cocktail w/stirrer, 6¼", 16 oz., w/lip	27.50	Tumbler, 11 oz., water, 4⅝"	12.00
Cocktail shaker w/lid	25.00	Tumbler, 16 oz., iced tea, 6½"	16.00
Cup	5.00	Vase, 8½", ruffled	37.50
Goblet, 4", 4½ oz., wine	10.00		

Please refer to Foreword for pricing information

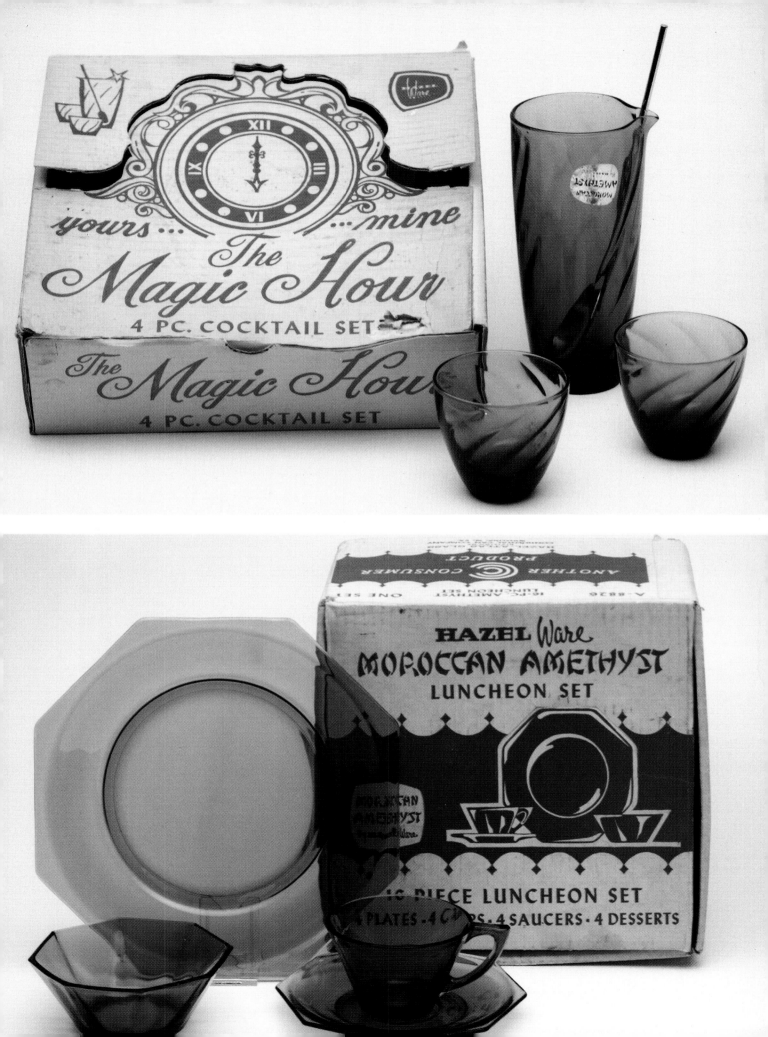

NAVARRE (Plate Etching #327) FOSTORIA GLASS COMPANY, 1937-1982

Colors: Crystal, blue, pink and rare in green.

Since the biggest distribution of this pattern was after 1937, I have chosen to include it in this book. Many of the harder to find pieces were made near the end of Fostoria's reign (late 1970's and early 1980's). Most of these pieces were signed "Fostoria" (acid etched on base) although some only carried a sticker. Some factory "seconds" sold through the outlet stores were not signed.

Prices for Navarre are higher on the West Coast; originally, retail prices in the West were higher due to shipping costs. In the price listing below, I have added the later pieces of Navarre as well as the colored items since they're being collected. A 1982 catalogue sheet is reprinted on page 137 that will display many of these pieces made right at the end of Navarre's production. You will find that accumulating a set of Navarre will be time consuming, but it can still be done.

	Crystal	Blue/Pink		Crystal	Blue/Pink
Bell, dinner	37.50	70.00	Plate, #2440, 10½" oval cake	47.50	
Bowl, #2496, 4", square, hndl.	11.00		Plate, #2496, 14", torte	57.50	
Bowl, #2496, 4⅜", hndl.	12.00		Plate, #2464, 16", torte	85.00	
Bowl, #869, 4½", finger	40.00		Relish, #2496, 6", 2 part, square	32.50	
Bowl, #2496, 4⅝", tri-cornered	15.00		Relish, #2496, 10" x 7½", 3 part	47.50	
Bowl, #2496, 5", hndl., ftd.	18.50		Relish, #2496, 10", 4 part	52.50	
Bowl, #2496, 6", square, sweetmeat	17.50		Relish, #2419, 13¼", 5 part	85.00	
Bowl, #2496, 6¼", 3 ftd., nut	18.50		Salt & pepper, #2364, 3¼", flat, pr.	55.00	
Bowl, #2496, 7⅜", ftd., bonbon	27.50		Salt & pepper, #2375, 3½", ftd., pr.	95.00	
Bowl, #2496, 10", oval, floating garden	50.00		Salad dressing bottle, #2083, 6½"	300.00	
Bowl, #2496, 10½", hndl., ftd.	62.50		Sauce dish, #2496, div. mayo., 6½"	37.50	
Bowl, #2470½, 10½", ftd.	55.00		Sauce dish, #2496, 6½" x 5¼"	125.00	
Bowl, #2496, 12", flared	60.00		Sauce dish liner, #2496, 8", oval	27.50	
Bowl, #2545, 12½", oval, "Flame"	55.00		Saucer, #2440	6.00	
Candlestick, #2496, 4"	20.00		Stem, #6106, ¾ oz., cordial, 3⅞"	47.50	
Candlestick, #2496, 4½", double	32.50		Stem, #6106, 3¼ oz., wine, 5½"	35.00	
Candlestick, #2472, 5", double	42.50		Stem, #6106, 3½ oz., cocktail, 6"	25.00	
Candlestick, #2496, 5½"	27.50		Stem, #6106, 4 oz., oyster cocktail, 3⅝"	27.50	
Candlestick, #2496, 6", triple	45.00		Stem, #6106, 4½ oz., claret, 6"	40.00	45.00
Candlestick, #2545, 6¾", double, "Flame"	48.00		Stem, #6106, 5 oz., continental		
Candlestick, #2482, 6¾", triple	50.00		champagne, 8⅛"	40.00	50.00
Candy, w/cover, #2496, 3 part	100.00		Stem, #6106, 6 oz., cocktail/sherry, 6³⁄₁₆"	35.00	
Celery, #2440, 9"	27.50		Stem, #6106, 6 oz., low sherbet, 4⅜"	24.00	
Celery, #2496, 11"	37.50		Stem, #6106, 6 oz., saucer champagne, 5⅝"	24.00	30.00
Comport, #2496, 3¼", cheese	27.50		Stem, #6106, 6½ oz., large claret, 6½"	37.50	45.00
Comport, #2400, 4½"	30.00		Stem, #6106, 10 oz., water, 7⅝"	30.00	37.50
Comport, #2496, 4¾"	30.00		Stem, #6106, 15 oz., brandy inhaler, 5½"	30.00	
Cracker, #2496, 11" plate	42.50		Stem, #6106, 16 oz., magnum, 7¼"	60.00	67.50
Creamer, #2440, 4¼", ftd.	20.00		Sugar, #2440, 3⅝", ftd.	18.00	
Creamer, #2496, individual	17.50		Sugar, #2496, individual	16.00	
Cup, #2440	18.00		Syrup, #2586, Sani-cut, 5½"	300.00	
Ice bucket, #2496, 4⅜" high	100.00		Tid bit, #2496, 8¼", 3 ftd., turned up edge	22.00	
Ice bucket, #2375, 6" high	140.00		Tray, #2496½, for ind. sugar/creamer	22.00	
Mayonnaise, #2375, 3 piece	67.50		Tumbler, #6106, 5 oz., ftd., juice, 4⅝"	25.00	
Mayonnaise, #2496½, 3 piece	67.50		Tumbler, #6106, 10 oz., ftd., water, 5⅜"	25.00	
Pickle, #2496, 8"	27.50		Tumbler, #6106, 12 oz., flat, highball, 4⅞"	36.00	
Pickle, #2440, 8½"	30.00		Tumbler, #6106, 13 oz., flat,		
Pitcher, #5000, 48 oz., ftd.	325.00		double old fashioned, 3⅝"	40.00	
Plate, #2440, 6", bread/butter	11.00		Tumbler, #6106, 13 oz., ftd., tea, 5⅞"	30.00	35.00
Plate, #2440, 7½", salad	15.00		Vase, #4108, 5"	75.00	
Plate, #2440, 8½", luncheon	20.00		Vase, #4121, 5"	75.00	
Plate, #2440, 9½", dinner	42.50		Vase, #4128, 5"	75.00	
Plate, #2496, 10", hndl., cake	47.50		Vase, #2470, 10", ftd.	145.00	

Please refer to Foreword for pricing information

Navarre

All items in the delicately etched Navarre Pattern are available in Crystal. Some items are not available in Blue. For specific information please refer to the Fostoria Price List.

Color Key:
NA01/Crystal
NA02/Blue

Navarre Blue Goblet

Multi-Purpose Navarre Magnums

Wilma Blue — Goblet
Wilma Crystal — Goblet
Navarre Crystal — Goblet
Low Dessert/Champagne
High Dessert/Champagne

Large Claret   Claret   Cordial   Magnum   Continental Champagne

Bell   7 in. Plate 8 in. Plate   Double Old Fashioned   High Ball

Luncheon Goblet/Ice Tea   Footed Juice   Brandy Inhaler   Cocktail/Sherry

1

NEW ERA #4044, A.H. HEISEY CO., 1934-1941; 1944-1957(stems, celery tray, and candlesticks)

Colors: Crystal, frosted crystal, some cobalt with crystal stem and foot.

Production of New Era was begun in the 1930's; but the stemware so often seen now fits this book's time frame. New Era is sought by "Art Deco" collectors. The double branched candelabra with the New Era bobeches is not hard to find, but very desirable. Dinner plates without scratches and after dinner cups and saucers will keep you searching for a long time unless you are lucky!

Note the cobalt stem below on the left. Any New Era stem with cobalt bowl will fetch $100.00 to $150.00. Keep that in mind in your travels. I might point out that luncheon plate with the label shown on the right. I left the label ("flower pot saucer") on the piece that I bought out of an antique mall in Indiana. I wonder who ever had <u>monogrammed</u> flower pot saucers? Sometimes a little chuckle will make your day when you are out shopping for glass!

	Crystal		Crystal
Ash tray or indiv. nut	30.00	Stem, 1 oz. cordial	45.00
Bottle, rye w/stopper	120.00	Stem, 3 oz. wine	35.00
Bowl, 11" floral	25.00	Stem, 3½ oz., high, cocktail	10.00
Candelabra, 2 lite w/2 #4044 bobeche & prisms	55.00	Stem, 3½ oz. oyster cocktail	10.00
Creamer	35.00	Stem, 4 oz. claret	15.00
Cup	10.00	Stem, 6 oz. sherbet, low	10.00
Cup, after dinner	50.00	Stem, 6 oz. champagne	12.50
Pilsner, 8 oz.	25.00	Stem, 10 oz. goblet	15.00
Pilsner, 12 oz.	30.00	Sugar	35.00
Plate, 5½" x 4½" bread & butter	12.00	Tray, 13" celery	30.00
Plate, 9"x 7", luncheon	20.00	Tumbler, 5 oz. ftd. soda	7.00
Plate, 10" x 8", dinner	35.00	Tumbler, 8 oz. ftd. soda	10.00
Relish, 13" 3-part	25.00	Tumbler, 10 oz., low, ftd.	10.00
Saucer	5.00	Tumbler, 12 oz. ftd. soda	12.50
Saucer, after dinner	10.00	Tumbler, 14 oz. ftd. soda	15.00

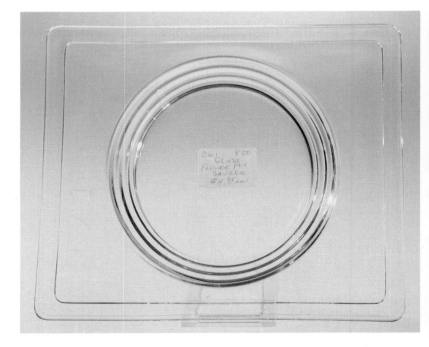

Please refer to Foreword for pricing information

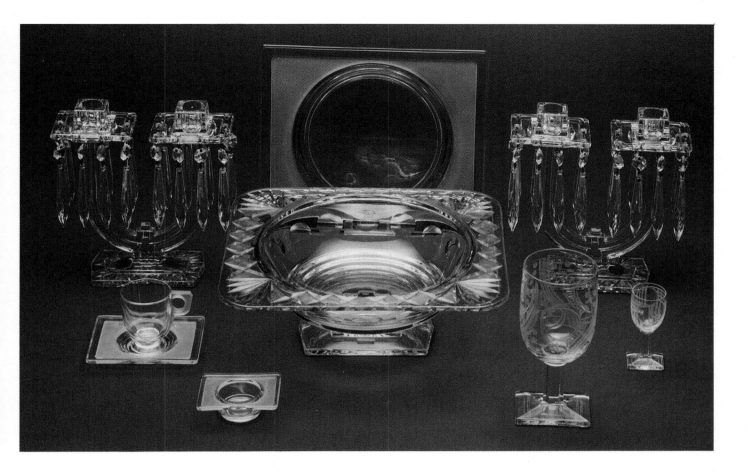

NEWPORT, "HAIRPIN" HAZEL ATLAS GLASS COMPANY, 1940-early 1950's

Colors: Platonite white and fired-on colors.

Newport is a pattern that Hazel Atlas made in the late 1930's in several transparent colors and afterward continued making as Platonite ware until the early 1950's. This splits the listing into both this book and *The Collector's Encyclopedia of Depression Glass*. The "Platonite" white and white with fired on colors was a popular line for Hazel Atlas. Notice the white edge on the fired-on pink plate in the rear. The edges and back of this plate are white. The pink or other colors decorates only the top. On the other hand, the turquoise blue bowl is a solid fired-on color without the white bottom.

The white color comes in two distinct shades. One is very translucent and the other is a flat white similar to what many collectors know as milk glass. The white shaker shown here is often used by Petalware collectors as shakers for their pattern since there are no shakers in the MacBeth-Evans set. It is not unusual for collectors to be fooled into thinking these shakers really are Petalware.

I just received a photograph of a couple of Newport fired-on blue tumblers that were found by a California lady at a flea market. She reports that she left a lone green one. Hopefully I will attain their measurements before this book is finally finished. If you have additional unlisted Platonite pieces, please let me know! Do not assume I already have information you can not find listed. I often learn new information from you collectors!

	White	Fired-on colors
Bowl, 4¾", berry	3.50	5.50
Bowl, 4¾", cream soup	5.50	8.50
Bowl, 8¼, large berry	9.50	13.00
Cup	3.50	6.00
Creamer	4.50	7.50
Plate, 6", sherbet	1.00	1.50
Plate, 8½", luncheon	3.00	5.00
Plate, 11½", sandwich	10.00	14.00
Platter, 11¾", oval	12.00	17.50
Salt and pepper, pr.	18.00	22.50
Saucer	.75	1.00
Sherbet	3.50	6.00
Sugar	4.50	7.50
Tumbler		12.00

OVIDE, incorrectly dubbed "NEW CENTURY" HAZEL ATLAS GLASS COMPANY, 1930-1950's

Colors: Green, black, white Platonite trimmed and fired-on colors in 1950's.

Ovide is another Hazel Atlas pattern that started in the Depression era, but continued being made until the 1950's. The photo on the right shows pastel banded Platonite that was used in restaurants and competed with Anchor Hocking's Jade-ite Restaurant Ware line. To date, there is little collector interest in the Platonite with pastel banded edges. More often, this inexpensively priced glassware is being gathered to be used as everyday dishes. It works well in both the microwave and the dishwasher according to collectors who are using it that way. Those two facts alone should attract more customers. If it doesn't go in the dishwasher, Cathy doesn't allow it in our kitchen!

The bottom of page 142 shows the most desirable decorations in this pattern. This photo was included again because a reader told me that her Goose decorated set was a wedding present in 1942. The 40's Goose line had already been photographed with the 30's Art Deco when I received that information as I worked on the first book. Since I am using that photograph again, I will also price the Art Deco here. Afterwards, it will only be in *The Collector's Encyclopedia of Depression Glass*. I still have seen only one Deco sugar and creamer priced for sale in all my travels. I purchased those years ago, but I have been unable to purchase any of the other pieces shown in that photograph.

One of the difficulties in ordering glass through the mail is miscommunication between buyer and seller. I ordered an eighteen piece set of dark "Moderntone" colors through the mail several years ago expecting to receive Moderntone pattern. I got Moderntone Ovide. The box is pictured at the bottom of 143 and the contents are shown at the top of the page. (The ash tray set was acquired separately.) If I had phoned the lady again and mailed the box back, I would have lost several dollars in the transaction; so I kept the box of dishes never realizing that someday it would come in handy as reference material. Evidently, **MODERNTONE** referred to the **colors and not the pattern**. In any case, the box says that it includes an eighteen piece breakfast set in burgundy, chartreuse, green and gray. This "green" will probably cause some confusion to Moderntone (pattern) collectors because "green" is the actual color designation by Hazel Atlas for that color collectors have always called forest or dark green. Every old dog does have to learn new tricks!

Prices can be found on the top of page 142.

OVIDE, incorrectly dubbed "NEW CENTURY" (Cont.)

	White w/trims	Decorated White	Fired-on Colors	Art Deco
Ash tray, square			4.00	
Bowl, 4¾", berry	3.50	6.50	5.50	
Bowl, 5½", cereal, deep		14.00		
Bowl, 8", large berry			18.00	
Creamer	4.50	16.00	5.50	77.50
Cup	3.50	12.50	4.50	47.50
Plate, 6", sherbet	1.50	2.50		
Plate, 8", luncheon	2.50	13.00	4.00	42.50
Plate, 9", dinner	3.50			
Platter, 11"	7.50	24.00		
Refrigerator stacking set, 4 pc.		47.50		
Salt and pepper, pr.	13.00			
Saucer	1.00	2.50		17.50
Sherbet	5.50	2.00		42.50
Sugar, open	4.50	17.50	5.50	77.50
Tumbler		18.00		77.50

PANELED GRAPE PATTERN #1881 WESTMORELAND GLASS COMPANY, 1950-1970's

Colors: White and white w/decorations.

Paneled Grape was one of Westmoreland's most successful patterns. When introduced in 1950, the few pieces made quickly gave way to more until over a hundred pieces were produced. Several dealers from both the East and West coasts helped in pricing this particular pattern that I have sold little of in my shop. I have bought and sold older glass for years and it is difficult to change one's ways.

Most of these listings were provided by friends, and the catalogue pages shown on pages 147-149 are from a 1973 catalogue. Note the birds, flowers and fruit decorations. Many non-collectors have these hanging on walls, just because they like them. It is one of those patterns you either love or hate. Some people are turned off by white milk glass; and if this is not your "thing," there are plenty of other patterns in this time period to suit your fancy. Collect what gives you pleasure!

	White, w/decorations		White, w/decorations
Appetizer or canapé set, 3 pc. (9" three-part relish/round fruit cocktail/ladle)	62.50	Candy jar, 3 ftd., w/cover	32.50
Basket, 5½", ruffled	52.50	Candy jar, 6¼", w/cover	25.00
Basket, 6½", oval	25.00	Canister, 7"	110.00
Basket, 8"	77.50	Canister, 9½"	130.00
Basket, 8", ruffled	62.50	Canister, 11"	155.00
Bon bon, 8", ruffled w/metal handle	50.00	Celery or spooner, 6"	40.00
Bottle, 5 oz., toilet	62.50	Cheese/old fashioned butter, 7", round w/cover	57.50
Bottle, oil or vinegar, w/stopper, 2 oz.	22.00	Chocolate box, 6½", w/cover	52.50
Bowl, pedestal base, 5" (used w/12"/12½" lipped/10" rnd. bowls & epergne)	65.00	Compote, 4½", crimped	30.00
Bowl, 4", crimped	22.00	Compote, 7" covered, ftd.	47.50
Bowl, 6", crimped, stemmed	30.00	Compote, 9" ftd., crimped	77.50
Bowl, 6", ruffled edge, stemmed	30.00	Condiment set, 5 pc. (oil and vinegar, salt and pepper on 9" oval tray)	100.00
Bowl, 6½" x 12½", 3⅛" high	110.00	Creamer, 6½ oz.	16.00
Bowl, 6½", oval	23.00	Creamer, individual	11.00
Bowl, 8", cupped	38.00	Creamer, large (goes w/lacy edge sugar)	22.50
Bowl, 8½", shallow	55.00	Creamer, small	10.00
Bowl, 9", ftd., 6" high, skirted base	47.50	Cup, coffee, flared	13.00
Bowl, 9", ftd., w/cover	67.50	Cup, punch, cupped	12.00
Bowl, 9", lipped	100.00	Decanter, wine	130.00
Bowl, 9", lipped, ftd.	100.00	Dresser set, 4 pc. (2)5 oz. toilet bottles, puff box and 13½" oval tray	200.00
Bowl, 9", square, w/cover	35.00	Egg plate, 12"	75.00
Bowl, 9½", bell shape	45.00	Egg tray, 10", metal center handle	57.50
Bowl, 9½", ftd., bell shaped	100.00	Epergne vase, 8½", bell	55.00
Bowl, 10", oval	37.50	Epergne vase, pattern at top	175.00
Bowl, 10½", round	77.50	Epergne set, 2 pc. (9" lipped bowl/8½" epergne vase)	107.50
Bowl, 11", oval, lipped, ftd.	100.00	Epergne set, 2 pc. (11½" epergne flared bowl/8½" epergne vase)	107.00
Bowl, 11½", oval, ruffled edge	77.50	Epergne set, 2 pc. (12" epergne lipped bowl/8½" epergne vase)	185.00
Bowl, 12", lipped	110.00	Epergne set, 2 pc. (14" flared bowl/8½" epergne vase)	210.00
Bowl, 12" ftd., banana	120.00		
Bowl, 12½", bell shape	120.00	Epergne set, 3 pc. (12" epergne lipped bowl/5" bowl base/8½" epergne vase)	300.00
Bowl, 13", punch, bell or flared	275.00	Epergne set, 3 pc. (14" flared bowl/5" bowl base/8½" epergne vase)	285.00
Bowl, 14", shallow, round	140.00	Flower pot	47.50
Bowl, ftd., ripple top	70.00	Fruit cocktail, 3½" w/6" sauce plate, bell shape	22.50
Butter w/cover, ¼ pound	22.00	Fruit cocktail, 4½" w/6" sauce plate, round	25.00
Cake salver, 10½"	65.00	Ivy ball	47.50
Cake salver, 11", round ftd., w/skirt	70.00	Jardiniere, 5", cupped and ftd.	25.00
Canapé or set, 3 pc. (12½" canapé tray/3½" cocktail/ladle)	120.00	Jardiniere, 5", straight sided	25.00
Candelabra, 3 lite, ea.	250.00	Jardiniere, 6½", cupped and ftd.	35.00
Candle holder, 4", octagonal, pr.	27.50		
Candle holder, 5", w/colonial hdld.	35.00		
Candle holder, 8", 2 lite (4 of these form a circular center piece)	32.50		

Please refer to Foreword for pricing information

PANELED GRAPE PATTERN #1881 (Cont.)

	White, w/decorations		White, w/decorations
Jardiniere, 6½", straight sided	35.00	Sauce boat	30.00
Jelly, 4½", covered	27.50	Sauce boat tray, 9"	30.00
Ladle, small	10.00	Saucer	8.50
Ladle, punch	57.50	Sherbet, 3¾", low foot	16.00
Lighter in 2 oz. goblet	30.00	Sherbet, 4¾", high foot	17.50
Lighter in tooth pick	33.00	Soap dish	77.50
Marmalade, w/ladle	57.50	Stem, 2 oz. cordial or wine goblet	22.50
Mayonnaise set, 3 pc. (round fruit cocktail/6" sauce plate/ladle)	35.00	Stem, 3 oz.	30.00
Mayonnaise, 4", ftd.	27.50	Stem, 5 oz., wine goblet	30.00
Napkin ring	17.50	Stem, 8 oz. water goblet	18.00
Nappy, 4½", round	14.00	Sugar w/cover, lacy edge on sugar to serve as spoon holder	32.50
Nappy, 5", bell shape	22.00	Sugar, 6½"	14.00
Nappy, 5", round w/handle	30.00	Sugar, small w/cover	14.00
Nappy, 7", round	30.00	Tid-bit or snack server, 2 tier (dinner and breakfast plates)	65.00
Nappy, 8½", round	30.00	Tid-bit tray, metal handle on 8½" breakfast plate	27.50
Nappy, 9", round, 2" high	40.00	Tid-bit tray, metal handle on 10½" dinner plate	47.50
Nappy, 10", bell	45.00	Toothpick	24.00
Parfait, 6"	23.00	Tray, 9", oval	45.00
Pedestal, base to punch bowl, skirted	160.00	Tray, 13½", oval	77.50
Pickle, oval	21.00	Tumbler, 5 oz. juice	24.00
Pitcher, 16 oz.	47.50	Tumbler, 6 oz. old fashioned cocktail	27.50
Pitcher, 32 oz.	37.50	Tumbler, 8 oz.	22.50
Planter, 3" x 8½"	35.00	Tumbler, 12 oz. ice tea	25.00
Planter, 4½", square	40.00	Vase, 4", rose	20.00
Planter, 5" x 9"	38.00	Vase, 4½, rose, ftd., cupped, stemmed	35.00
Planter, 6", small, wall	67.50	Vase, 6", bell shape	20.00
Planter, 8", large, wall	110.00	Vase, 6½" or celery	35.00
Plate, 6", bread	14.00	Vase, 8½", bell shape	25.00
Plate, 7" salad, w/depressed center	25.00	Vase, 9", bell shape	25.00
Plate, 8½", breakfast	22.00	Vase, 9", crimped top	32.00
Plate, 10½", dinner	45.00	Vase, 9½", straight	35.00
Plate, 14½"	110.00	Vase, 10" bud (size may vary)	20.00
Plate, 18"	150.00	Vase, 11", rose (similar to bud vase but bulbous at bottom)	35.00
Puff box or jelly, w/cover	27.50	Vase, 11½", bell shape	47.50
Punch set, 15 pc. (13" bowl, 12 punch cups, pedestal and ladle)	560.00	Vase, 11½", straight	35.00
Punch set, 15 pc. (same as above w/11" bowl w/o scalloped bottom)	479.00	Vase, 12", hand blown	150.00
Relish, 9", 3 part	39.50	Vase, 14", swung (size varies)	19.00
Salt and pepper, 4¼", small, ftd., pr.	22.50	Vase, 15"	30.00
*Salt and pepper, 4¼", small, ftd., pr.,	27.50	Vase, 16", swung (size varies)	20.00
Salt and pepper, 4½", large, flat, pr.	50.00	Vase, 18", swung (size varies)	20.00

*All over pattern

Please refer to Foreword for pricing information

"Panel Grape"
GIFT SUGGESTIONS TO PLEASE THE DISCRIMINATING

1881
Bowl, Crimp.

1881 Bowl.
Lip. Ftd.

1881 Bowl.
Shallow

1881
Basket, Hld.

1881
Bowl, Lip.

1881
Bowl, Oval

1881/6½"
Basket

1881
Appetizer Set

1881
Bowl, Bell

1881
Bowl, Rose

1881
Butter

1881
Bon Bon

3

147

FAMOUS *"Panel Grape"* THE COLLECTORS FAVORITE

1881 Plates, 14½″, 10½″ & 8½″

1881
3 pc. Canister Set

1881
Jug, Qt.

1881
Salver, Skirted

1881
Salver, Ftd.

1881 Snack Server

1881
Egg Tray

1881
Ice Tea

1881
Goblet

1881
Sauce Boat/Tray

1881
Mayonnaise

1881
Condiment Set

1881
Salt/Pepper,
Lg.

1881
Oil

1881
Salt/Pepper
(Min. 3 Sets)

1881
Candy

1881
Dish, 3 Ftd.

1881
Puff Box/
Jelly

1881
Chocolate Box

1881
Candy, Crimp.

1881
Pickle

4

1881
Starter Set

1881
Candlestick

1881
Mayo
Set

1881
Cup/Saucer

1881
Dish, Oval

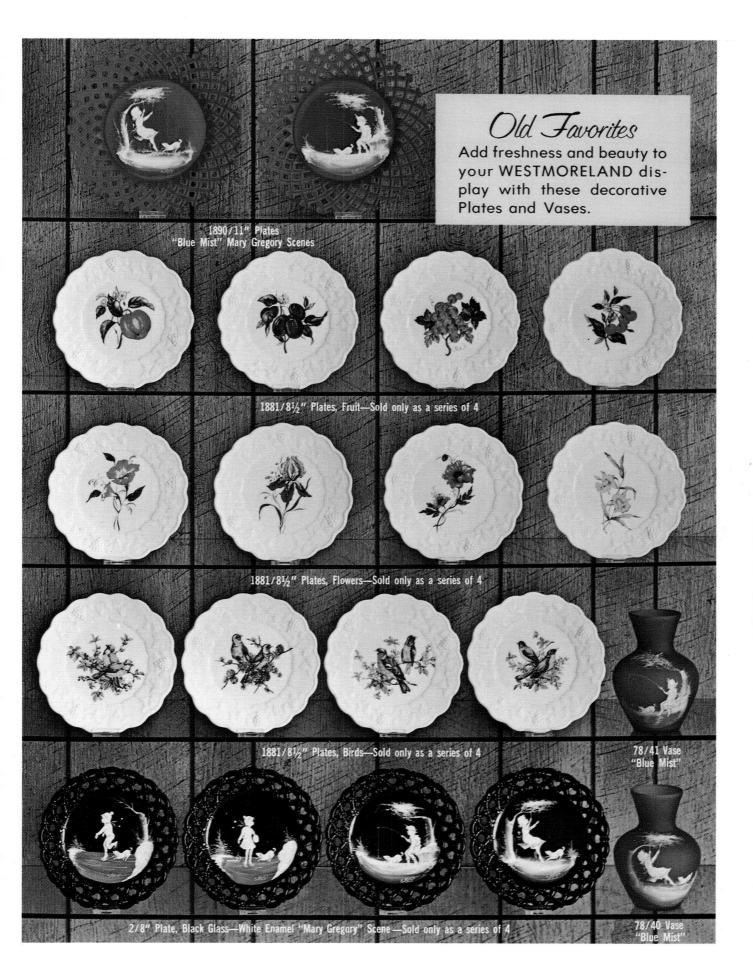

Old Favorites

Add freshness and beauty to your WESTMORELAND display with these decorative Plates and Vases.

1890/11" Plates
"Blue Mist" Mary Gregory Scenes

1881/8½" Plates, Fruit—Sold only as a series of 4

1881/8½" Plates, Flowers—Sold only as a series of 4

1881/8½" Plates, Birds—Sold only as a series of 4

78/41 Vase
"Blue Mist"

2/8" Plate, Black Glass—White Enamel "Mary Gregory" Scene—Sold only as a series of 4

78/40 Vase
"Blue Mist"

MGT0731
Plate, 14½"

MGT0730
Plate, 10½"

MGT0734
Sauce Boat

MGT0729
Plate, 8½"

MGT0737
Sugar & Cream, Small

MGT0724
Cup & Saucer

MGT0733
Salt & Pepper
Small, Height, 4¼"

MGT0721
Appetizer Set

MGT0726
Jug, 1 Qt.

MGT0725
Goblet

MGT0736
Sugar & Cream,
Large

MGT0722
Butter

MGT0732
Salt & Pepper
Large, Height, 4½"

MGT0739
Wine

MGT0738
Tid Bit Tray

Milk Glass Tableware

1881
Sauce Boat/Tray

1881
Goblet
8 oz.

1881
Sugar/Cream, Lg.

1881
Jug, Qt.

1881 Salt/Pepper

large

small

1881 Oil, 2 oz.

small

1881 Sugar/Cream

1881
Snack
Server

1881
Tid Bit
Tray

1881
Appetizer
Set

1881
Marmalade
W/Ladle

1881 Plate, 14½"

1881 Plate, 10½"

1881 Plate, 8½"

1881
Cheese

1881 Butter

1881 Cup/Saucer

29

109
Cookie Jar

...Kitchen & Table Accessories

Collector's items from the vast "Paneled Grape" pattern

1881/9"
Bowl, Sq.

1881/9"
Compote, Crimped

1881
Compote, Crimped

1881/7"
Compote

1881
Candy Jar

1881
Decanter

1881
Celery/Vase

1881
Dish, 3 Ftd.

1881
Chocolate Box

1881
Candleholder

1881
Cocktail, Fruit

1881
Cheese

1881/9"
Bowl, Bell

1881/¼ #
Butter

1881
Cup/Saucer

1881
Candle

1881
Dish

1881/12"
Bowl, Lipped

1881
Bowl, Banana

1881
Bowl, Oval Lpd.

Excellent Gift Suggestions in a treasured pattern

1881/14½"
Plate

1881/10½"
Plate

1881/8½"
Plate

1881/6"
Plate

1881
Mayonnaise

1881/2 oz.
Oil

1881/4½"
Nappy

1881
Ice Tea

1881
Goblet

1881/1 Pt.
Jug

1881/1 Qt.
Jug

1881/6½"
Jardiniere

1881/5"
Jardiniere

1881
Pickle

1881
Mayo Set

1881
Puff Box/Jelly

1881
Flower Pot

1881
Planter, Oblong

1881
Planter, Window

1881
Planter, Sq.

1881
Ivy Ball

Exquisite Reproductions from choice Originals

1881/15″
Vase

1881/2/11½″
Vase

1881/9″
Vase

1881/8½″
Vase

1881
Vase, Rose

1881
Vase, Blown

1881/18″
Vase

1881/6″
Vase

1881
Vase, Bud

1881
Sauce Boat/Tray

1881
Sugar/Cream

1881/1
Sugar/Cream

1881
Snack Server

1881/11″
Cake Salver

1881/10½″
Cake Salver

1881
Soap

1881
Salt/Pepper Set

1881
Wine

1881
Sherbet

1881
Sugar/Cream, Ind.

1881
Tumbler

1881
Toothpick

FAMOUS PANELED GRAPE THE MILK GLASS COLLECTOR'S FAVORITE

1881
Decanter

1881
Jug, Pt.

1881
Jug, Qt.

1881
Dish, 3 Ftd.

1881/9"
Compote, Crimp.

1881/4½"
Compote, Crimp.

1881
Goblet

1881
Ice Tea

1881
Compote

1881
Candy

1881
Celery/Vase

1881
Flower Pot

1881
Candlestick

1881
Condiment Set

1881
Candy, Crimp.

1881
Canape Server

1881
Cheese

1881
Choc. Box

1881 Dish, Oval

1881 Wine

1881 Cup/Saucer

1881 Cocktail, Fruit

13

1881
15 Pc. Punch Set
(Ind. Boxed)

1881
Pickle

1881
Snack Server

1881
Sauce Boat/Tray

1881
Oil

1881
Salt/Pepper, Lg.

1881
Cake Salver
(Ind. Boxed)

1881
Planter, Obl.

1881
Puff Box/Jelly

1881
Salt/Pepper
(Packed 3 Sets Per Box)

1881
Mayonnaise

1881
Mayo Set

1881/10½"
Plate
14½" Plate Also Available

1881/8½"
Plate

1881/6"
Plate

14

GIFT SUGGESTIONS TO PLEASE THE MOST DISCRIMINATING

1881/15"
Vase

1881/9"
Vase, Crimp.

1881/9"
Vase

1884/9"
Bowl, Fld.
(Ind. Boxed)

1881/6"
Vase

1881/8½"
Vase

1881
Vase, Bud

1881
Vase, Rose

1884/5"
Bowl, Fld.

1884/7"
Bowl, Sq.

1881
Sugar/Cream, Ind.

1881
Sugar/Cream

1881
Toothpick
(6 per box)

1881/1
Sugar/Cream

1884/6½"
Ash Tray

1884/5"
Ash Tray

1884/4"
Ash Tray

1884/4" Bowl, Sq.

15

PARK AVENUE FEDERAL GLASS COMPANY, 1941-early 1970's

Colors: Amber, crystal and crystal w/gold trim.

This smaller line of Federal has been brought into several glass shows for me to identify. The trademark of **F** in a shield is embossed on the bottom of most of the pieces. Federal used the Star pitchers shown on page 183 with the tumblers from this set. They made no Park Avenue pitcher, per se.

All the pieces listed were made into the early 1960's except the shot glass that was in production until the early 1970's. Notice that the catalogue spells whisky without the "e" which is considered a British spelling today. Amber is harder to find and the gold trimmed crystal pieces are prone to the gold wearing off. This pattern is one of the smaller sized sets shown in this book and would make an ideal beginning pattern.

	Amber/Crystal
Ash tray, 3½", square	5.00
Ash tray, 4½", square	7.00
Bowl, 5", dessert	5.00
Bowl, 8½", vegetable	10.00
Tumbler, 2⅛", 1¼ oz., whisky	4.00
Tumbler, 3½", 4½ oz., juice	5.00
Tumbler, 3⅜", 9 oz.	6.00
Tumbler, 4¾", 10 oz.	6.50
Tumbler, 5⅛", 12 oz., iced tea	7.50

Please refer to Foreword for pricing information

PRESSED TUMBLERS

Matching lines . . . such as the famed Park Avenue on this page, or the Star Line on the next . . . new, unusual shapes, and standard staples, are shown here in Federal's selection of pressed tumblers. All are designed and engineered for eye-appeal, serviceability, and good value.

PARK AVENUE TUMBLERS

1122 — 1¼ oz.
PARK AVENUE WHISKY
Ht. 2⅛"
Pkd. 12 doz. ctn. Wt. 16 lbs.

1122 — 4½ oz.
PARK AVENUE JUICE TUMBLER
Ht. 3½"
Pkd. 12 doz. ctn. Wt. 35 lbs.

1122 — 9 oz.
PARK AVENUE TUMBLER
Ht. 3⅞"
Pkd. 12 doz. ctn. Wt. 56 lbs.

1142—10 oz.
PARK AVENUE TUMBLER*
Ht. 4¾"
Pkd. 6 doz. ctn. Wt. 37 lbs.

1122 — 12 oz.
PARK AVENUE ICED TEA
Ht. 5⅛"
Pkd. 6 doz. ctn. Wt. 43 lbs.

*CK 1142—10 oz. PARK AVENUE TUMBLER IN CARRY-KITS
are available factory-packed: 6 tumblers to each
Carry-Kit, 12 kits to ctn. Wt. 40 lbs.

19

"PRETZEL," No. 622 INDIANA GLASS COMPANY, Late 1930's-1980's

Colors: Crystal, teal and avocado with recent issues in amber and blue.

Pretzel is another of Indiana's numbered patterns (No. 622) which is better known by its collectors' name. The 4½" fruit cup has been found on a plate that has a 1¼" tab handle. This tab handled plate measures 6" according to all the letters I received (after mentioning that I did not own one to measure in an earlier book.) It seems numerous collectors own this plate and I appreciate their information.

That dated 1955 blue plate with "Virgo" astrology sign found in North Carolina has also generated much mail. Most collectors have written to say that they have found some astrology sign other than "Virgo," but a lady in California has a full set! These seem to be selling in the $4.00 to 5.00 range according to readers, although some have been purchased for as little as a quarter! Evidently, these were a special order or promotional gimmick. If you find out, let me know!

Embossed fruit in the center of Pretzel is now selling for twenty-five to fifty per cent more than the plain centered pieces. Only a few collectors are buying these, but be aware that there is a much smaller supply of fruit centers than the plain centered Pretzel. Some fruit centered pieces are even color decorated, and that does add to their appeal.

Pitcher and tumblers are still sparsely found. Although there are three sizes of tumblers, none are easily located. Those tumblers, along with a pitcher, are shown in the insert on page 161.

Have any of you found any more teal Pretzel? I would like to know if you have any in your collections. The cup shown here is still the only piece that I have seen! Have you seen a saucer?

	Crystal
Bowl, 4½", fruit cup	4.50
Bowl, 7½", soup	10.00
Bowl, 9⅜", berry	16.00
Celery, 10¼", tray	1.50
Creamer	4.50
*Cup	6.00
Olive, 7", leaf shape	5.00
Pickle, 8½", two hndl.	5.50
Pitcher, 39 oz.	155.00
Plate, 6"	2.50
Plate, 6", tab hndl.	3.00
Plate, 7¼", square, indent	9.00
Plate, 7¼", square, indent 3-part	9.00
Plate, 8⅜", salad	6.00
Plate, 9⅜", dinner	10.00
Plate, 11½", sandwich	11.00
**Saucer	1.00
Sugar	4.50
Tumbler, 5 oz., 3½"	22.00
Tumbler, 9 oz., 4½"	24.00
Tumbler, 12 oz., 5½"	32.00

* Teal - $30.00
** Teal - $10.00

ROMANCE ETCHING #341, FOSTORIA GLASS COMPANY, 1942–1986

Color: Crystal.

Romance has often been confused with June because of the "bow" in the design, so be sure to compare the shapes of Romance to June. Romance only comes in crystal; thus, the only confusion occurs with crystal. Any colored piece of Fostoria with a "bow" has to be June by default. Pricing Romance has been a problem because of regional differences. In some areas it is considered too new to be highly priced, while in other areas it is considered as good as June. Here is a compilation of several collectors and dealers pricing ideas! Remember, this book's pricing is to be considered only a guide.

	Crystal		Crystal
Ash tray, 2⅝", indiv., #2364	12.50	Plate, 11", sandwich, #2364	35.00
Bowl, 6", baked apple #2364	15.00	Plate, 11¼", cracker, #2364	22.50
Bowl, 8", soup, rimmed, #2364	25.00	Plate, 14", torte, #2364	40.00
Bowl, 9", salad, #2364	37.50	Plate, 16", torte, #2364	55.00
Bowl, 9¼", ftd. blown, #6023	65.00	Plate, crescent salad, #2364	40.00
Bowl, 10", 2 hdld, #2594	42.50	Relish, 8", pickle, #2364	22.50
Bowl, 10½", salad, #2364	40.00	Relish, 10", 3 pt., #2364	25.00
Bowl, 11", shallow, oblong, #2596	45.00	Relish, 11", celery, #2364	27.50
Bowl, 12", ftd. #2364	55.00	Salt & pepper, 2⅝", pr., #2364	45.00
Bowl, 12", lily pond, #2364	45.00	Saucer, #2350	5.00
Bowl, 13", fruit, #2364	50.00	Stem, 3⅞", ¾ oz., cordial, #6017	42.50
Bowl, 13½", hdld., oval, #2594	55.00	Stem, 4½", 6 oz., low sherbet, #6017	14.00
Candlestick, 4", #2324	17.50	Stem, 4⅞", 3½ oz., cocktail, #6017	21.50
Candlestick, 5", #2596	22.50	Stem, 5½", 3 oz., wine, #6017	30.00
Candlestick, 5½", #2594	25.00	Stem, 5½", 6 oz., champagne, #6017	17.50
Candlestick, 5½", 2 lite, #6023	30.00	Stem, 5⅞", 4 oz., claret, #6017	35.00
Candlestick, 8", 3 lite, #2594	42.50	Stem, 7⅜", 9 oz., goblet, #6017	25.00
Candy w/lid, rnd., blown, #2364	77.50	Sugar, 3⅛", ftd., #2350½	16.50
Cigarette holder, 2", blown, #2364	35.00	Tray, 11⅛", ctr. hdld., #2364	32.50
Comport, 3¼", cheese, #2364	22.50	Tumbler, 3⅝", 4 oz., ftd., oyster cocktail, #6017	17.50
Comport, 5", #6030	22.50	Tumbler, 4¾", 5 oz., ftd., #6017	17.50
Comport, 8", #2364	37.50	Tumbler, 5½", 9 oz., ftd., #6017	21.00
Creamer, 3¼", ftd., #2350½	17.50	Tumbler, 6", 12 oz., ftd., #6017	27.50
Cup, ftd., #2350½	20.00	Vase, 5", #4121	35.00
Ice tub, 4¾", #4132	57.50	Vase, 6", ftd. bud, #6021	35.00
Ladle, mayonnaise, #2364	5.00	Vase, 6", ftd., #4143	45.00
Mayonnaise, 5", #2364	22.50	Vase, 6", grnd. bottom, #2619½	45.00
Pitcher, 8⅞", 53 oz., ftd., #6011	225.00	Vase, 7½", ftd., #4143	60.00
Plate, 6", #2337	8.00	Vase, 7½", grnd. bottom, #2619½	60.00
Plate, 6¾", mayonnaise liner, #2364	10.00	Vase, 9½", grnd. bottom, #2619½	85.00
Plate, 7", #2337	10.00	Vase, 10", #2614	75.00
Plate, 8", #2337	15.00	Vase, 10", ftd., #2470	95.00
Plate, 9", #2337	45.00		

Please refer to Foreword for pricing information

ROYAL RUBY ANCHOR HOCKING GLASS COMPANY, 1938-1960's; 1977

Color: Ruby red.

Although manufacture of Royal Ruby was begun in 1938, most of what is considered Royal Ruby was made after 1940. You will find a Royal Ruby section in my eleventh edition of *Collector's Encyclopedia of Depression Glass* covering the pieces made in the 1930's. Speaking of the 1930's, I found a catalogue page that shows the 6⅛"x4" "card holder" was listed as a cigarette box that came with four Royal Ruby ash trays. It is the most difficult piece to find in this pattern. Royal Ruby will continue to be listed in both books as it fits into both pre 1940 and post 1940 time periods.

Royal Ruby is the **Anchor Hocking** name for their red color. Only red glassware **produced by Hocking or Anchor Hocking** can be called Royal Ruby. It is a patented name that can only be used by them! A sticker was placed on each red piece designating it as Royal Ruby no matter what pattern it was. Red Bubble or Sandwich did not mean anything but Royal Ruby to the factory. So, if you find a red piece that seems to be some other **Hocking** pattern, do not be surprised by the Royal Ruby sticker.

There were six or seven sizes of beer bottles made for a national beer company in 1949, 1950 and 1963. The date of manufacture is embossed on the bottom of each bottle. You will find '49, '50 or '63 on these bottles. Pictured are 32 ounce (1949), 7 ounce (1959) and 12 (1963) ounce bottles. Millions of these bottles were made, but they were too costly and were discontinued. Bottle collectors seem to find these more attractive than Royal Ruby collectors and the quart bottles are being priced from $30.00 up at these shows. The quart size is the most commonly seen. I do not consider them dinnerware items, although some collectors might disagree!

Both sherbet styles are shown in front of the beer bottles. The stemmed version is behind the footed one. Oval vegetable bowls are scarce. Other items in short supply (besides the alias "card holder"/cigarette box) are the three quart upright pitcher, punch bowl base, and the salad bowl with 13¾" underliner.

That upright 3 quart pitcher and the 5, 9 and 13 ounce flat tumblers were listed as the Roly-Poly Line in a 1951 catalogue. That page also shows the Royal Ruby Charm which became just Royal Ruby in future catalogues. As I mentioned under Charm on page 58, Forest Green and Royal Ruby square were not considered to be Charm in subsequent catalogues after they were introduced under that name.

I have also listed the crystal stems with Royal Ruby tops called "Boopie" by collectors and the stems that go with Royal Ruby Bubble. See a complete explanation under Bubble on page 14.

Hopefully, you will find this revised listing of Royal Ruby easier to use than previous listings in my earlier books.

	Red		Red
Ash tray, 4½", leaf	4.00	Plate, 13¾"	25.00
Beer bottle, 7 oz.	17.50	Punch bowl	40.00
Beer bottle, 12 oz.	22.50	Punch bowl base	37.50
Beer bottle, 16 oz.	35.00	Punch cup, 5 oz.	3.00
Beer bottle, 32 oz.	35.00	Saucer, round	2.50
Bowl, 4¼", round, fruit	5.50	Saucer, 5⅝", square	2.50
Bowl, 4¾", square, dessert	7.00	Sherbet, ftd.	8.00
Bowl, 5¼", popcorn	12.00	Sherbet, stemmed, 6½ oz.	8.00
Bowl, 7½", round, soup	12.50	*Stem, 3½ oz., cocktail	10.00
Bowl, 7⅜", square	13.00	*Stem, 4 oz., juice	10.00
Bowl, 8", oval, vegetable	37.50	Stem, 4½ oz., cocktail	10.00
Bowl, 8½", round, large berry	17.50	Stem, 5½ oz., juice	12.50
Bowl, 10", deep, popcorn (same as punch)	40.00	Stem, 6 oz., sherbet	8.00
Bowl, 11½", salad	32.50	*Stem, 6 oz., sherbet	8.00
Cigarette box/"card holder," 6⅛" x 4"	52.50	*Stem, 9 oz., goblet	14.00
Creamer, flat	8.00	Stem, 9½ oz., goblet	13.00
Creamer, ftd.	9.00	*Stem, 14 oz., iced tea	20.00
Cup, round	6.00	Sugar, flat	8.00
Cup, square	6.00	Sugar, ftd.	7.50
Goblet, ball stem	10.00	Sugar, lid	10.00
Ice bucket	35.00	Tumbler, 2½ oz., ftd. wine	13.00
Lamp	35.00	Tumbler, 3½ oz., cocktail	12.50
Pitcher, 3 qt., tilted	35.00	Tumbler, 5 oz., juice, ftd. or flat	7.50
Pitcher, 3 qt., upright	45.00	Tumbler, 9 oz., water	6.50
Pitcher, 42 oz., tilted or straight	30.00	Tumbler, 10 oz., 5", water, ftd.	6.50
Plate, 6¼", sherbet, round	4.00	Tumbler, 12 oz., 6" ftd., tea	15.00
Plate, 7", salad	5.00	Tumbler, 13 oz., iced tea	13.00
Plate, 7¾", salad, round	6.00	Vase, 4", ivy, ball-shaped	5.00
Plate, 8⅜", square	8.00	Vase, 6⅜, two styles	8.00
Plate, 9⅛", dinner, round	11.00	Vase, 9", two styles	17.50

* "Boopie"

Please refer to Foreword for pricing information

SANDWICH CRYSTAL ANCHOR HOCKING GLASS COMPANY, 1939-1964; 1977

Color: Crystal 1940-1960's.

I have split the **crystal** Anchor Hocking Sandwich from the **colors** to facilitate writing about each. Royal Ruby Sandwich will appear with Royal Ruby in the eleventh edition of *The Collector's Encyclopedia of Depression Glass.*

A newly discovered piece is the scalloped top 6½" cereal bowl shown in the top photo on 167 (behind the creamer and to the right of the normally found cereal.) A group of four was found in the Columbus, Ohio, area last year. Evidently, these scalloped edge pieces were a special order or a trial issue. This goes along with the scalloped rimmed plate shown as a pattern shot below! That heavy 9" plate with a scalloped rim is the only one I have seen; if you have some in your collection, let me know since this one bit the dust after our last photography session! The scalloped cereals have sold for $100.00.

Another new edition is the 7½" bowl shown on the far right of that picture. Notice the smaller scallops on this as compared to those normally found. There seem to be twice the number of scallops on this new find! Three sizes of scalloped bowls are shown sitting inside each other in the bottom photo.

Other crystal pieces that are infrequently found are the regular cereal, footed tumbler and the 5" crimped dessert bowl that is shown in a metal holder in the top picture. Metal attachments were usually manufactured outside the factory. Glassware was sold to some other company or individual who made holders or embellishments for these pieces!

That 5" crimped dessert listed by Anchor Hocking only measures 4⅞" in some cases. Mould variation makes size listings a major problem! Both this and the crimped sherbets are listed as occasional Sandwich pieces in the 1956 catalogue. "Crimped" is their word used to describe these occasional pieces.

Collecting Anchor Hocking's Sandwich continues to prosper while Indiana's Sandwich does not do as well. Hocking went to some trouble to preserve the collectability of their older glassware; however, Indiana did not. Prices continue to increase in this popular pattern. In fact, this may be the most collected crystal pattern in this book with the exception of Iris.

Remember that Anchor Hocking reintroduced a crystal cookie jar in the late 1970's that was much larger than the old. For a comparison of these cookie jars I am enclosing measurements. The newer one is currently selling in the $12.00 range.

	NEW	OLD
Height	10¼"	9¼"
Opening width	5½"	4⅞"
Circumference/largest part	22"	19"

Pieces in short supply continue to be found, but demand keeps absorbing these. My shop always has plenty of cups, saucers and 8" plates. These were premiums for buying $3.00 (about ten gallons) of gas at Marathon stations in 1964. We had quite a few of these free dishes when we married twenty-eight years ago. The promotion took four weeks for cups and saucers and the next four weeks for the plates. You could have gotten the crystal punch bowl set for only $2.89 with an oil change and lube! Ah, the "good old days"!

	Crystal			Crystal
Bowl, 4⁵⁄₁₆", smooth	5.00		Sugar	8.50
Bowl, 4⅞"/5", crimped dessert	15.00		Sugar cover	15.00
Bowl, 4⅞", smooth	6.00		Tumbler, 3⅜", 3 oz., juice	12.50
Bowl, 5¼", scalloped	7.50		Tumbler, 3⁹⁄₁₆", 5 oz., juice	6.50
Bowl, 6½", smooth	7.50		Tumbler, 9 oz., water	8.00
Bowl, 6½", scalloped, deep	7.50		Tumbler, 9 oz., footed	25.00
Bowl, 6¾", cereal	30.00			
Bowl, 7", salad	7.00			
Bowl, 7¼", scalloped	8.00			
Bowl, 8", scalloped	8.00			
Bowl, 8¼", oval	7.00			
Bowl, 9", salad	23.00			
Butter dish, low	45.00			
Butter dish bottom	25.00			
Butter dish top	20.00			
Cookie jar and cover	36.00			
Creamer	6.00			
Cup, tea or coffee	2.50			
Custard cup	3.50			
Custard cup, crimped, 5 oz.	12.50			
Custard cup liner	15.00			
Pitcher, 6", juice	55.00			
Pitcher, ½ gal., ice lip	70.00			
Plate, 7", dessert	9.50			
Plate, 8"	4.00			
Plate, 9", dinner	17.50			
Plate, 9", indent for punch cup	5.00			
Plate, 12", sandwich	12.50			
Punch bowl, 9¾"	18.00			
Punch bowl stand	24.00			
Punch cup	2.25			
Saucer	1.50			
Sherbet, footed	8.00			

Please refer to Foreword for pricing information

SANDWICH COLORS ANCHOR HOCKING GLASS COMPANY, 1939-1964

Colors: Desert Gold 1961-1964   Forest Green 1956-1960's   Pink 1939-1940
Royal Ruby 1938-1939   White/Ivory (opaque) 1957-1960's

Forest Green Sandwich continues to increase in price except for those five pieces that were packed in "Crystal Wedding" oats. Everyone ate oats; so there are virtually thousands of those five pieces available today. Prices for Forest Green have risen due to scarcity and demand! All known pieces of Forest Green are shown in the photograph. Thank you for reminding me the custard cup and liners were left out of the pricing list last time! Sorry, those two oatmeal pieces did not increase in price just because I left them out! I got a letter from a novice collector surmising they were rare since they were not listed.

Even new collectors seem to gravitate to the green. Perhaps the Forest Green Sandwich appears more desirable than the plain Forest Green that has numerous fans. Dinner plates at $85.00 do not seem to discourage many. I sell all I can find!

There appear to be more cups than saucers, so the prices for saucers are gradually increasing.

Pitchers in Forest Green are scarce because of poor marketing procedures. Everyone received the juice and water **tumblers** in oats as explained above. Juice and water sets were offered for sale with a pitcher and six tumblers. Everyone already had more than enough tumblers, so they would not buy the complete sets. Most of these sets were returned to Anchor Hocking unsold.

No Forest Green Sandwich sugar or cookie jar lids have ever been found. Employees remember those topless cookie jars being sold as vases. They must have convinced people that they were wonderful vases because so many are seen today!

I have priced the Royal Ruby Sandwich here, but it can also be found in *The Collector' Encyclopedia of Depression Glass* in the Royal Ruby section of that book.

Only pink bowls can be found; so there are few collectors of that color. Amber Sandwich is beginning to attract new collectors. However, the footed amber tumbler is nearly impossible to find! The rest of the set can be obtained with some work and patience. That flashed-on blue cup and saucer may have been a special order and there may be additional colors. As yet, I have not seen other objects with this treatment. Let me know what you find!

For only $2.89 you could buy the Ivory with gold trim punch bowl set with an oil change and lubrication at Marathon gas stations in my area in 1964. These punch sets were first made in 1957. They were made in Ivory and Ivory trimmed in 22K gold. There is little price differentiation today, but that set trimmed in gold seems to be less in demand because the gold has a tendency to wear when used!

	Desert Gold	Royal Ruby	Forest Green	Pink	Ivory/White
Bowl, 4 5/16", smooth			3.50		
Bowl, 4 7/8", smooth	3.00	16.00		4.00	
Bowl, 5 1/4", scalloped	6.00	20.00			
Bowl, 5 1/4", smooth				7.00	
Bowl, 6 1/2", smooth	6.00				
Bowl, 6 1/2", scalloped		27.50	37.50		
Bowl, 6 3/4", cereal	12.00				
Bowl, 7", salad			55.00		
Bowl, 8", scalloped		40.00	65.00	16.00	
Bowl, 9", salad	27.50				
Cookie jar and cover	35.00		*17.50		
Creamer			25.00		
Cup, tea or coffee	3.50		19.00		
Custard cup			1.50		
Custard cup liner			1.50		
Pitcher, 6", juice			125.00		
Pitcher, 1/2 gal., ice lip			350.00		
Plate, 9", dinner	9.00		85.00		
Plate, 12", sandwich	14.00				
Punch bowl, 9 3/4"					15.00
Punch bowl stand					15.00
Punch cup					2.00
Saucer	3.00		12.00		
Sugar, no cover			25.00		
Tumbler, 3 9/16", 5 oz., juice			4.00		
Tumbler, 9 oz., water			5.00		
Tumbler, 9 oz., footed	100.00				

* no cover

Please refer to Foreword for pricing information

SANDWICH INDIANA GLASS COMPANY, 1920's-1980's

Colors: Crystal late 1920's-Today   Teal Blue 1950's-1980's   Milk White- mid 1950's
     Amber late 1920's-1980's   Red 1933/1969-early 1970's   Smokey Blue 1976-1977

Indiana's Sandwich pattern is dearly loved by some collectors. Still, other collectors and many dealers avoid it due to the company's propensity for reissuing the glass. This procedure never allows their older glassware to attain the age status that other companies' glassware has. Pink and green Sandwich will be priced in the eleventh *Collector's Encyclopedia of Depression Glass* since they were made in the 1930's; and although green (now called Chantilly) has been made again, it is a different shade than the original. The older green will glow under an ultraviolet (black) light if you have one available!

Tiara Exclusives took over Sandwich from Indiana with an issue of red in 1969, amber in 1970 and crystal in 1978. Amber, Chantilly green and crystal were made into the late 1980's.

Basically, the list below incorporates the original Sandwich line from the 1920's and the original Tiara listings from the late 1960's and early 1970's. Eventually, I may add all the Tiara listings throughout the 1970's and 1980's, but only **if** they become collectible. So far, I've seen little evidence of this.

The mould for the old wine broke and a new one was designed. All the wines made in the last few years are fatter (like Iris cocktails) than the earlier ones which were shaped like Iris wines. These older wines are 4½" tall and hold 3 oz. The newer wines are shown in Tiara catalogues but no measurements for size or capacities are given. If you own one, please send me the measurements to pass along.

Teal blue and milk glass (white) are colors issued in the 1950's; but Tiara remade a teal butter dish as an "exclusive" hostess gift that ravaged the $200.00 price tag on the old butter dish. This new one originally sold for approximately $15.00. "New" Sandwich has been touted to prospective customers as glass that's going to be valuable based on its past performance—and the company is destroying the collectability of the older glassware by selling new glass copies!

Six items in red Sandwich date from 1933, i.e., cups, saucers, luncheon plates, water goblets, creamers and sugars. Many of these pieces are inscribed 1933 Chicago World's Fair. In 1969, Tiara Home Products produced red pitchers, 9 oz. goblets, cups, saucers, wines, wine decanters, 13" serving trays, creamers, sugars, salad and dinner plates. There is little difference in pricing unless you have some red Sandwich marked 1933 Chicago World's Fair. This older, marked glass will bring more due to its being a World's Fair collectible.

Amber and crystal prices are shown, but you must realize that most of the crystal and all the amber have been made since 1970. Prices below reflect the small amounts of these colors that I see at flea markets, malls, etc. Usually the seller is a former Tiara "Party Plan" hostess who is disposing of leftover wares.

	Amber Crystal	Teal Blue	Red		Amber Crystal	Teal Blue	Red
Ash trays (club, spade, heart, dmd. shapes, ea.)	3.50			Goblet, 9 oz.	13.00		45.00
Basket, 10", high	32.50			Mayonnaise, ftd.	13.00		
Bowl, 4¼", berry	3.50			Pitcher, 68 oz.	22.50		150.00
Bowl, 6"	4.00			Plate, 6", sherbet	3.00	7.00	
Bowl, 6", hexagonal	5.00	14.00		Plate, 7", bread and butter	4.00		
Bowl, 8½"	11.00			Plate, 8", oval, indent for sherbet		6.00	12.00
Bowl, 9", console	16.00			Plate, 8⅜", luncheon	5.00		20.00
Bowl, 11½", console	19.00			Plate, 10½", dinner	8.00		
Butter dish and cover, domed	22.50	*155.00		Plate, 13", sandwich	13.00	25.00	35.00
Butter dish bottom	6.00	42.50		Puff box	16.50		
Butter dish top	16.50	112.50		Salt and pepper, pr.	16.50		
Candlesticks, 3½", pr.	17.50			Sandwich server, center handle	18.00		47.50
Candlesticks 7", pr.	25.00			Saucer	2.25	6.00	7.00
Creamer	9.00		45.00	Sherbet, 3¼"	5.50	12.00	
Celery, 10½"	16.00			Sugar, large	9.00		45.00
Creamer and sugar on diamond shaped tray	16.00	32.00		Sugar lid for large size	13.00		
Cruet, 6½ oz. and stopper		135.00		Tumbler, 3 oz., footed cocktail	7.50		
Cup	3.50	8.00	27.50	Tumbler, 8 oz., footed water	9.00		
Decanter and stopper	22.50		85.00	Tumbler, 12 oz., footed tea	10.00		
				Wine, 3", 4 oz.	6.00		12.50

*Beware recent vintage sells for $20.00

Please refer to Foreword for pricing information

SHELL PINK MILK GLASS JEANNETTE GLASS CO., 1957-1959

Color: Opaque pink.

Prices for Shell Pink have made some leaps in the last two years! All pieces that were hard to find then have become even more difficult with all the new collectors searching for the pattern. This popular Jeannette pattern was made only for a short period in the late 1950's. It was called Shell Pink and included pieces from several popular Jeannette lines hoping to enhance its commercial success. Shell Pink was designed as "a delicate coloring that blends perfectly with all kinds of flowers. Its smooth satiny finish goes all the way through the glass — is not a spray or surface coating."

The quotes above are from a four page catalogue from Jeannette. These pages also state "Shell Pink Milk Glass' lovely color and design make women admire it — and buy it!" Today, there may be as many men searching for this colored glassware as women.

I will point out a few original prices for your information: cookie jar and cover, $1.10; lazy susan, $2.00; butterfly cigarette set (box and two trays) $1.00; heavy bottom vase, $0.75 and finally the 12-piece punch set, $4.00 with extra cups at $1.25 dozen. The lazy susan was packed one to a pink gift box similar to the blue one shown under Dewdrop on page 44.

The photograph on top of page 173 shows a variety of pieces. The 9" heavy bottom vase shown in the center remains one of the most difficult pieces to find. The Gondola fruit bowl by Jeannette is the long, handled bowl (on the right behind the round powder jar and in front of the square candy dish). The oval footed bowl on the left is called a Lombardi bowl and was used with a pair of double candle holders shown in front of it. Those two covered bowls on the left are called wedding bowls. The bowl in the right foreground is the Florentine bowl and the one on the left is the Vineyard 12" relish.

The elusive lazy susan is shown in the top photo on page 174; the base is the part that is almost non-existent, but original ball bearings to turn the trays are not easily found either. Some collectors have bought Dewdrop lazy susans just to get the ball bearings for their Shell Pink set. The bottom photograph shows the pieces made for "Napco Ceramics, Cleveland, Ohio." Each piece is marked thus with the numbers quoted in the price list except for the piece with a saw tooth edge in the back which only has "Napco, Cleveland." The piece in the front is the candy bottom of a pattern Jeannette called National which was made only in crystal in the late 1940's. This Shell Pink candy bottom was promoted as a vase.

At the top of page 175 pieces of other patterns in this book are shown and all the pieces that depict animals, insects and birds. The "Eagle" candle holder looks more like the same bird on the "Pheasant" bowl — not so according to Jeannette. That cigarette box with the butterfly finial is rather hard to find in mint condition. The price below is for **mint** condition butterfly boxes. The bottom of page 175 shows Thumbprint designed pieces and a pattern I am calling "Feather" that is like the punch bowl listed in the catalogue as "Feather" design. The snack tray, snack or punch cup, 15¾" tray, Venetian tray, and punch bowl all fit this pattern. Speaking of the punch bowl reminds me that the original ladle was **pink** plastic and not crystal. Those "Hostess" snack sets were rather expensive at the time. A set of four was $1.75. These were a new fad for the TV trays so abundant at the time.

	Opaque Pink		Opaque Pink
Ash tray, butterfly shape	15.00	"Napco" #2255, ftd. bowl w/saw tooth top	25.00
Base, for lazy susan, w/ball bearings	95.00	"Napco" #2256, square comport	12.50
Bowl, 6½", wedding, w/cover	22.50	"National" candy bottom	10.00
Bowl, 8", Pheasant, ftd.	35.00	Pitcher, 24 oz., ftd., Thumbprint	27.50
Bowl, 8", wedding, w/cover	25.00	Powder jar, 4¾", w/cover	30.00
Bowl, 9", ftd., fruit stand, Floragold	25.00	Punch base, 3½", tall	25.00
Bowl, 10", Florentine, ftd.	25.00	Punch bowl, 7½ qt.	50.00
Bowl, 10½", ftd., Holiday	40.00	Punch cup, 5 oz. (also fits snack tray)	6.00
Bowl, 10⅞", 4 ftd., Lombardi, designed center	40.00	Punch ladle, pink plastic	8.00
Bowl, 10⅞", 4 ftd., Lombardi, plain center	25.00	Punch set, 15 pc. (bowl, base, 12 cups, ladle)	155.00
Bowl, 17½", Gondola fruit	25.00	Relish, 12", 4 part, octagonal, Vineyard design	40.00
Cake stand, 10", Harp	30.00	Stem, 5 oz., sherbet, Thumbprint	10.00
Candle holder, 2 light, pr.	35.00	Stem, 8 oz., water goblet, Thumbprint	12.50
Candle holder, Eagle, 3 ftd., pr.	65.00	Sugar cover	13.00
Candy dish w/cover, 6½" high, square	30.00	Sugar, ftd., Baltimore Pear design	10.00
Candy dish, 4 ftd., 5¼", Floragold	20.00	Tray, 7¾" x 10", snack w/cup indent	9.00
Candy jar, 5½", 4 ftd., w/cover, grapes	18.00	Tray, 12½" x 9¾", 2 hndl., Harp	50.00
Celery and relish, 12½", 3 part	45.00	Tray, 13½", lazy susan, 5 part	40.00
Cigarette box, butterfly finial	90.00	Tray, 15¾", 5 part, 2 hndl.	40.00
Compote, 6", Windsor	20.00	Tray, 16½", 6 part, Venetian	30.00
Cookie jar w/cover, 6½" high	80.00	Tray, lazy susan complete w/base	125.00
Creamer, Baltimore Pear design	14.00	Tumbler, 5 oz., juice, ftd., Thumbprint	8.00
Honey jar, beehive shape, notched cover	35.00	Vase, 5", cornucopia	15.00
"Napco" #2249, cross hatch design pot	15.00	Vase, 7"	35.00
"Napco" #2250, ftd. bowl w/berries	15.00	Vase, 9", heavy bottom	65.00

Please refer to Foreword for pricing information

SILVER CREST FENTON ART GLASS COMPANY, 1943-PRESENT

Color: White with crystal edge.

Silver Crest is one of Fenton's longest production patterns. Every time they have dropped it out of manufacture, demand forces them to reissue it. There are ways to help date your pieces. Before 1958, the white was called opal and has an opalescence to it if you hold it up to the light. In 1958, a formula change to milk glass makes the glass look very white without "fire" in the white. Any pieces reintroduced after 1973 will be signed Fenton. Fenton began signing Carnival pieces in 1971 and in 1973 they continued this practice with all pieces. If you run into pieces that have white edging outside the crystal, this was called Crystal Crest and dates from 1942.

The punch bowl set and the hurricane lamps continue to be very desirable but difficult to acquire. You may not have ascertained this from the $10.00 listing instead of $100.00 in the first book! Sorry about that! Those decimal points have a way of haunting old mathematics teachers!

There are pieces of Silver Crest with two different line numbers. Originally, this line was #36 and all pieces carried that designation. In July 1952, Fenton began issuing a "Ware Number" for each piece. That is why you see two different numbers for some of the items.

See page 46 for prices on Emerald Crest. Aqua Crest has a blue edge and prices run between that of Silver Crest and Emerald Crest.

	White		White
Basket, 5" hndl., (top hat) #1924	37.50	Candle holder, low, ruffled, pr. #7271	20.00
Basket, 5", hndl. #680	37.50	Candle holder, ruffled comport style, pr. #7272	52.50
Basket, 6½", hndl. #7336	37.50	Candy box #7280	67.50
Basket, 7" #7237	27.50	Candy box, ftd., tall stem #7274	110.00
Basket, 12" #7234	45.00	Chip and dip (low bowl w/mayo in center) #7303	65.00
Basket, 13" #7233	75.00	Comport, ftd. #7228	11.00
Basket, hndl. #7339	60.00	Comport, ftd., low #7329	18.00
Bon bon, 5½" #7225	11.00	Creamer, reeded hndl. #680	16.00
Bon bon, 8" #7428	11.00	Creamer, reeded hndl. (same as #680) #7201	16.00
Bonbon, 5½" #36	11.00	Creamer, ruffled top	45.00
Bowl, 5½", soup #680	32.50	Creamer, straight side #1924	32.50
Bowl, 5", finger or deep dessert #680	26.00	Creamer, threaded hndl. #680	17.50
Bowl, 7" #7227	18.00	Cup, reeded hndl. #680, 7209	22.50
Bowl, 8½" #7338	32.50	Cup, threaded look hndl. #680	22.50
Bowl, 8½" flared #680	32.50	Epergne set, 2 pc. (vase in ftd. bowl) #7202	55.00
Bowl, 9½" #682	46.00	Epergne set, 3 pc. #7200	110.00
Bowl, 10" #7224	46.00	Epergne set, 6 pc. #1522/951	110.00
Bowl, 10" salad #680	46.00	Epergne, 2 pc. set #7301	77.50
Bowl, 11" #5823	46.00	Epergne, 4 pc. bowl w/3 horn epergnes #7308	110.00
Bowl, 13" #7223	46.00	Epergne, 5 pc. bowl w/4 horn epergnes #7305	110.00
Bowl, 14" #7323	46.00	Lamp, hurricane #7398	150.00
Bowl, banana, high ft. w/upturned sides #7324	65.00	Mayonnaise bowl #7203	11.00
Bowl, banana, low ftd. #5824	47.50	Mayonnaise ladle #7203	5.00
Bowl, deep dessert #7221	32.50	Mayonnaise liner #7203	27.50
Bowl, dessert, shallow #680	32.50	Mayonnaise set, 3 pc. #7203	45.00
Bowl, finger or dessert #202	18.00	Nut, ftd. #7229	10.00
Bowl, ftd., (like large, tall comport) #7427	67.50	Nut, ftd. (flattened sherbet) #680	10.00
Bowl, ftd., tall, square #7330	67.50	Oil bottle #680	80.00
Bowl, low dessert #7222	26.00	Pitcher, 70 oz. jug #7467	175.00
Bowl, shallow #7316	46.00	Plate, 5½" #680	6.00
Cake plate, 13" high, ftd. #7213	46.00	Plate, 5½", finger bowl liner #7218	6.00
Cake plate, low ftd. #5813	37.50	Plate, 6" #680	6.50
Candle holder, 6" tall w/crest on bottom, pr. #7474	70.00	Plate, 6½" #680, 7219	14.00
Candle holder, bulbous base, pr. #1523	27.50	Plate, 8½" #680, 7217	27.50
Candle holder, cornucopia, pr. #951	57.50	Plate, 10" #680	37.50
Candle holder, cornucopia (same as #951), pr. #7274	57.50	Plate, 10½" #7210	37.50
		Plate, 11½" #7212	37.50
Candle holder, flat saucer base, pr. #680	20.00	Plate, 12" #680	47.50
		Plate, 12" #682	47.50

Please refer to Foreword for pricing information

SILVER CREST (Cont.)

	White		White
Plate, 12½" #7211	47.50	Tid-bit, 3 tier, ruffled bowl #7397	85.00
Plate, 16", torte 7216	55.00	Top hat, 5" #1924	47.50
Punch bowl #7306	225.00	Tray, sandwich #7291	27.50
Punch bowl base #7306	65.00	Tumbler, ftd. #7342	47.50
Punch cup #7306	12.00	Vase, 4½" #203	11.00
Punch ladle (clear) #7306	22.50	Vase, 4½" #7254	11.00
Punch set, 15 pc. #7306	450.00	Vase, 4½", double crimped #36, #7354	11.00
Relish, divided #7334	32.50	Vase, 4½", fan #36	11.00
Relish, heart, hndl. #7333	22.50	Vase, 5" (top hat) #1924	46.00
Saucer #680, #7209	5.00	Vase, 6" #7451	16.00
Shaker, pr. #7206	100.00	Vase, 6", doubled crimped #7156	19.00
Sherbert #680	10.00	Vase, 6¼", double crimped #36, #7356	17.50
Sherbet #7226	10.00	Vase, 6¼", fan #36	17.50
Sugar, reeded hndl. #680	17.50	Vase, 7" #7455	17.50
Sugar, reeded hndl. (same as #680) #7201	17.50	Vase, 8" #7453	17.50
Sugar, ruffled top	45.00	Vase, 8", bulbous base #186	46.00
Sugar, sans hndls. #680	32.50	Vase, 8", doubled crimped #7258	22.00
Tid-bit, 2 tier (luncheon/dessert plates) #7296	47.50	Vase, 8", wheat #5859	42.50
Tid-bit, 2 tier (luncheon/dinner plates) #7294	47.50	Vase, 8½" #7458	47.50
Tid-bit, 2 tier plates #680	47.50	Vase, 9" #7454	47.50
Tid-bit, 2 tier, ruffled bowl #7394	75.00	Vase, 9" #7459	47.50
Tid-bit, 3 tier (luncheon/dinner/dessert plates) #7295	47.50	Vase, 10" #7450	110.00
Tid-bit, 3 tier plates #680	47.50	Vase, 12" (fan topped) #7262	100.00

SQUARE NO. 3797 CAMBRIDGE GLASS COMPANY, 1952-mid 1950's

Colors: Crystal, some red and black.

Cambridge Square is shown in the 1949 Cambridge catalogue as patent pending. This is one of the few patterns made by Cambridge that completely falls into the time span of this book.

A few pieces of Square were made in color, but some Carmen pieces were made by Imperial in the late 1960's. Carmen pieces by Cambridge are rarely seen, but the red from Imperial can be found with some work. The "crackle" tumbler shown in the back left of the bottom photograph sells for $50.00. There were several sizes of Square stemware made in Crackle.

	Crystal		Crystal
Ash tray, 3½" #3797/151	7.00	Plate, 9½", tidbit #3797/24	20.00
Ash tray, 6½" #3797/150	9.00	Plate, 11½" #3797/26	25.00
Bon bon, 7" #3797/164	13.50	Plate, 13½" #3797/28	30.00
Bon bon, 8" #3797/47	24.00	Relish, 6½", 2 part #3797/120	17.50
Bowl, 4½", dessert #3797/16	11.00	Relish, 8", 3 part #3797/125	22.50
Bowl, 6½", individual salad #3797/27	13.50	Relish, 10", 3 part #3797/126	25.00
Bowl, 9", salad #3797/49	320.00	Salt and pepper, pr. #3797/76	22.50
Bowl, 10", oval #3797/48	23.00	Saucer, coffee #3797/17	7.00
Bowl, 10", shallow #3797/81	27.50	Saucer, tea #3797/15	7.00
Bowl, 11", salad #3797/57	37.50	Stem, #3798, 5 oz., juice	10.00
Bowl, 12", oval #3797/65	30.00	Stem, #3798, 12 oz., iced tea	12.00
Bowl, 12", shallow #3797/82	35.00	Stem, #3798, cocktail	17.50
Buffet set, 4 pc. (plate, div. bowl, 2 ladles) #3797/29	47.50	Stem, #3798, cordial	25.00
Candle holder, 1¾", block #3797/492, pr.	22.50	Stem, #3798, sherbet	11.00
Candle holder, 2¾", block #3797/493, pr.	25.00	Stem, #3798, water goblet	12.00
Candle holder, 3¾", block #3797/495, pr.	26.00	Stem, #3798, wine	20.00
Candle holder, cupped #3797/67, pr.	25.00	Sugar #3797/41	10.00
Candy box and cover #3797/165	30.00	Sugar, individual #3797/40	10.00
Celery, 11" #3797/103	23.00	Tray, 8", oval, for individual sug/cr #3797/37	17.50
Comport, 6" #3797/54	22.50	Tumbler, #3797, 5 oz., juice	12.50
Creamer #3797/41	10.00	Tumbler, #3797, 14 oz., iced tea	17.50
Creamer, individual #3797/40	10.00	Tumbler, #3797, low cocktail	12.00
Cup, coffee, open handle #3797/17	10.00	Tumbler, #3797, low cordial	27.50
Cup, tea, open handle #3797/15	10.00	Tumbler, #3797, low sherbet	10.00
Decanter, 32 oz. #3797/85	80.00	Tumbler, #3797, low wine	15.00
Ice tub, 7½" #3797/34	32.50	Tumbler, #3797, water goblet	13.50
Icer, cocktail w/liner #3797/18	32.50	Vase, 5", belled #3797/92	22.50
Lamp, hurricane, 2 pc. #3797/68	40.00	Vase, 5½", belled #3797/91	25.00
Mayonnaise set, 3 pc. (bowl, plate, ladle) #3797/129	30.00	Vase, 6" #3797/90	22.50
Oil bottle, 4½ oz. #3797/100	20.00	Vase, 7½", ftd. #3797/77	22.50
Plate, 6", bread and butter #3797/20	8.00	Vase, 7½", rose bowl #3797/35	33.00
Plate, 7", dessert or salad #3797/23	12.00	Vase, 8", ftd. #3797/80	20.00
Plate, 7", salad #3797/27	11.00	Vase, 9½", ftd. #3797/78	27.50
Plate, 9½", dinner or luncheon #3797/25	27.50	Vase, 9½", rose bowl #3797/36	42.50
		Vase, 11", ftd. #3797/79	37.50

STAR FEDERAL GLASS COMPANY, 1950's

Colors: Amber, crystal and crystal w/gold trim.

This smaller Federal pattern is just now beginning to show up in the collecting arena. Although there were not many pieces made, you can put together a reasonably priced set of this pattern. Notice the "star" shaped design on each piece as displayed in the photograph. You will have to look at the catalogue information sheet on page 183 to see the pitcher styles. I did not find one until after the photography session; you will have one to view in the next photo shoot.

Note that the whisky is spelled without the "e" in the original catalogue listing.

	Amber/Crystal
Bowl, 4⅝", dessert	4.00
Bowl, 8⅜", vegetable	9.00
Pitcher, 5¾", 36 oz., juice	8.00
Pitcher, 7", 60 oz.	12.00
Pitcher, 9¼", 85 oz., ice lip	15.00
Plate, 6³⁄₁₆" salad	3.00
Plate, 9⅜", dinner	5.00
Tumbler, 2¼", 1½ oz., whisky	3.00
Tumbler, 3⅜" 4½ oz., juice	4.00
Tumbler, 3⅞", 9 oz., water	5.50
Tumbler, 5⅛", 12 oz., iced tea	7.50

PRESSED TUMBLERS

1123 — 1½ oz.
STAR WHISKY
Ht. 2¼"
Pkd. 12 doz. ctn. Wt. 17 lbs.

1123 — 4½ oz.
STAR JUICE TUMBLER
Ht. 3⅜"
Pkd. 12 doz. ctn. Wt. 37 lbs.

1123 — 9 oz.
STAR TUMBLER
Ht. 3⅞"
Pkd. 12 doz. ctn. Wt. 56 lbs.

1123 — 12 oz.
STAR ICED TEA
Ht. 5⅛"
Pkd. 6 doz. ctn. Wt. 42 lbs.

2844 — 36 oz.
STAR JUICE JUG
Ht. 5¾"
Pkd. 2 doz. ctn. Wt. 37 lbs.

(Also available — 2845-60 oz. JUG
Ht. 7" Pkd. 1 doz. ctn. Wt. 26 lbs.)

2846 — 85 oz.
STAR ICE LIP JUG
Ht. 9¼"
Pkd. 1 doz. ctn. Wt. 38 lbs.

1116 — 5 oz.
PANEL JUICE TUMBLER
Ht. 3⅜"
Pkd. 12 doz. ctn. Wt. 38 lbs.

1116 — 9 oz.
PANEL TUMBLER
Ht. 4"
Pkd. 12 doz. ctn. Wt. 59 lbs.

1116 — 12 oz.
PANEL ICED TEA
Ht. 5⅜"
Pkd. 6 doz. ctn. Wt. 43 lbs.

1131 — 9 oz.
CATHEDRAL TUMBLER
Ht. 4"
Pkd. 12 doz. ctn. Wt. 58 lbs.

STARS and STRIPES ANCHOR HOCKING GLASS GLASS COMPANY, 1942

Color: Crystal.

I have been asked questions about this little pattern for years. Most collectors seemed to think that these pieces were Queen Mary, but this proves conclusively that it is a completely different pattern named appropriately "Stars and Stripes." As I wrote about this for the first book, we were welcoming home Desert Storm troops, but this time we are dropping bombs on Iraq again. The missing sherbet will make it in the photograph next book. I promise! Some people are very frantic in their search for this since it appeared in my book.

	Crystal
Plate, 8"	12.00
Sherbet	13.00
Tumbler, 5", 10 oz.	25.00

Stars and Stripes DESSERT SERVICE IN SPARKLING CRYSTAL

EARLY AMERICAN DESIGN

SHERBET ★ 5¢
TUMBLER ★ 5¢
PLATE ★ ★ 10¢

My lunch box
"life-savers"
...the tempting, nutritious
KRAFT CHEESE SPREADS
Kraft Pineapple
Kraft Pimento
Kraft Olive-Pimento
Kraft Relish Spread
Kraft Limburger Spread
Old English Spread
Kraft American Spread
The zestful Roka
Kraft Pimento American Spread
KRAFT CHEESE COMPANY
MANUFACTURER
CHICAGO, ILLINOIS
5 OZS. NET WGT.
KRAFT
PIMENTO
CHEESE SPREAD
VARIETY for those daily lunch box sandwiches! Flavor goodness, and wholesome nutrition, too. The nine famous Kraft Cheese Spreads give you all this, and for a *bargain* in ration points. Remember, the quality Kraft Spreads are *dairy* products... wholesome, good. Use them often.
Copr. 1943 by Kraft Cheese Company
The World's Favorite Cheeses are made by KRAFT

SWANKY SWIGS 1930's-1950's

Swanky Swigs were originally packed with a Kraft cheese product in them. Illustrated here are the Swigs produced from the late 1930's into the 1950's with a 1976 bicentennial also shown. Smaller size glasses and the larger 10 oz. sizes seem to have only been issued in Canada. The limited availability of these sizes in the states makes their prices continue to soar. Tulip No. 2 only turns up on the West Coast and prices are a little less there. Earlier Swanky Swigs can be found in *The Collector's Encyclopedia of Depression Glass* if you get hooked on collecting these. Lids from these tumblers are shown on page 189 as is the plate offered on one lid "for a quarter and two jar labels from Kraft Cheese Spreads." Lids fetch $5.00 up depending upon condition and advertisement! The plate sells in the $2.00 to $3.50 range. Apparently, many of these labels were redeemed since there are so many of these plates available today.

Page 187:

Row 1: Tulip No. 1	blue	4½"	12.50-15.00
	blue	3½"	3.00-4.00
	red	4½"	12.50-15.00
	red	3½"	3.00-4.00
	green	4½"	12.50-15.00
	green, black	3½"	3.00-4.00
	green w/label	3½"	8.00-10.00
Tulip No. 2	red, green	3½"	20.00-25.00
Row 2: Tulip No. 2	black	3½"	20.00-25.00
Carnival	yellow, red	3½"	4.00-6.00
	green, blue	3½"	4.00-6.00
Tulip No. 3	lt. blue, yellow	3¾"	2.50-3.50
	dk. blue	4½"	12.50-15.00
	dk blue	3¾"	2.50-3.50
	dk. blue	3¼"	7.50-10.00
Row 3: Tulip No. 3	red	4½"	12.50-15.00
	red	3¾"	2.50-3.50
Posey: Tulip	red	4½"	12.00-15.00
	red	3½"	3.00-4.00
Posey: Jonquil	yellow	4½"	12.00-15.00
	yellow	3½"	4.00-5.00
Posey: Violet	purple	4½"	12.50-15.00
	purple	3½"	4.00-5.00
	purple	3¼"	7.50-10.00
Row 4: Cornflower No. 1	lt. blue	4½"	12.50-15.00
	lt. blue	3½"	4.00-5.00
	lt. blue	3¼"	7.50-10.00
Cornflower No. 2	dk. blue	3½"	2.50-3.50
	lt. blue	3½"	2.50-3.50
	lt. blue	3¼"	7.50-10.00
	red, yellow	3½"	2.50-3.50
	yellow	3¼"	7.50-10.00

Page 188

Row 1: Forget-Me-Not	dk. blue, blue, red, yellow	3½"	2.00-3.00
	yellow w/label	3½"	8.00-10.00
	yellow	3¼"	7.50-10.00
Daisy	red, white & green	4½"	12.50-15.00
	red, white & green	3¾"	2.00-3.00
Daisy	red & white	3¾"	20.00-25.00
Row 2: Bustling Betsy	all colors	3¾"	3.00-4.00
	all colors	3¼"	7.50-10.00
Row 3: Antique Pattern: all designs		3¾"	3.00-4.00
clock & coal scuttle brown; lamp & kettle blue; coffee grinder & plate green; spinning wheel & bellows red; coffee pot & trivet black; churn & cradle orange		3¼"	7.50-10.00
Kiddie Cup: cat and rabbit green		4½"	12.50-15.00
		3¾"	3.00-4.00
Row 4: Kiddie Cup: all designs		3¼"	7.50-10.00
bird & elephant red; bear & pig blue; squirrel & deer brown; duck & horse black; dog & rooster orange		3¾"	3.00-4.00
bird & elephant w/label		3¾"	8.00-10.00
dog & rooster **w/cheese**		3¾"	25.00-30.00
Bicentennial issued in 1975; yellow, red, green		3¾"	3.00-5.00

Please refer to Foreword for pricing information

A Publication I recommend:

DEPRESSION GLASS DAZE

THE ORIGINAL NATIONAL DEPRESSION GLASS NEWSPAPER

Depression Glass Daze, the original, national monthly newspaper dedicated to the buying, selling and collecting of colored glassware of the 20's and 30's. We average 60 pages each month, filled with feature articles by top-notch columnists, readers' "finds," club happenings, show news, a china corner, a current listing of new glass issues to be aware of and a multitude of ads! You can find it in the **DAZE**! Keep up with what's happening in the dee gee world with a subscription to the **DAZE**. Buy, sell or trade from the convenience of your easy chair.

Name _____ Street _____

City _____ State _____ Zip _____

☐1 Year - $21.00   ☐Check Enclosed   ☐Please bill me

☐Mastercard   ☐Visa   (Foreign subscribers - Please add $1.00 per year)

Card No. _____ Exp. Date _____

Signature _____

Send to: D.G.D., Box 57GF, Otisville, MI 48463-0008 - Please allow 30 days

Other Books By Gene Florence

Kitchen Glassware of the Depression Years, 4th Edition......................$19.95
Pocket Guide to Depression Glass, 8th Edition....................................$9.95
Collector's Encyclopedia of Akro Agate...$14.95
Collector's Encyclopedia of Depression Glass 11th Edition...................$19.95
Collector's Encyclopedia of Occupied Japan I....................................$14.95
Collector's Encyclopedia of Occupied Japan II...................................$14.95
Collector's Encyclopedia of Occupied Japan III..................................$14.95
Collector's Encyclopedia of Occupied Japan IV..................................$14.95
Collector's Encyclopedia of Occupied Japan V...................................$14.95
Elegant Glassware of the Depression Era, V.......................................$19.95
Very Rare Glassware of the Depression Years I....................................$24.95
Very Rare Glassware of the Depression Years II...................................$24.95
Very Rare Glassware of the Depression Years III.................................$24.95
The Standard Baseball Card Price Guide, 6th Edition.........................$9.95

Collector's Encyclopedia of Depression Glass 11th edition

by Gene Florence

America's No. 1 bestselling glass book is bigger and better than ever. Depression glass collecting is at an all-time high as shown by the sales of the 10th edition. The all-new revised edition will be no exception with many new finds being added plus many new photos to bring out the best possible detail for each pattern. Over 5,000 pieces are photographed in full color with complete descriptions and current values included for each piece. A special section is included exposing re-issues and fakes, alerting the buyer as to what has been released and how to determine old valuable glass from worthless new issues. Gene Florence is America's most respected authority on this period glassware and has sold well over 1,000,000 copies of his popular glass books. This encyclopedia is no exception. It will once again be a bestseller.

No dealer, glass collector or investor can afford not to own this book.

8½x11", 224 pages HB..$19.95

Schroeder's Antiques Price Guide

Schroeder's Antiques Price Guide has become THE household name in the antiques & collectibles field. Our team of editors works year around with more than 200 contributors to bring you our #1 bestselling book on antiques & collectibles.

With more than 50,000 items identified & priced, *Schroeder's* is a must for the collector & dealer alike. If it merits the interest of today's collector, you'll find it in *Schroeder's*. Each subject is represented with histories and photos are used each year to illustrate not only the rare and unusual, but the everyday "fun-type" collectibles as well—not postage stamp pictures, but large close-up shots that show important details clearly.

Our editors compile a new book each year. Never do we merely change prices. Each category is thoroughly checked to spot inconsistencies, listings that may not be entirely reflective of actual market dealings, and lines too vague to be of merit. Only the best of the lot remains for

publication. You'll find *Schroeder's Antiques Price Guide* the one to buy for factual information and quality.

8½x11", 608 pages, PB $12.95